CRICKET'S LIGHTER SIDE

A CRICKETER COLLECTION

EDITED BY
Christopher Martin-Jenkins

SIMON & SCHUSTER

LONDON • SYDNEY • NEW YORK • TOKYO • TORONTO

First published in Great Britain by
Simon & Schuster Ltd in 1988

Copyright © The Cricketer 1988

Simon & Schuster Ltd
West Garden Place
Kendal Street
London W2 2AQ

Simon & Schuster of Australia Pty Ltd
Sydney

British Library Cataloguing-in-Publication Data available

ISBN 0-671-69958-X

Made by Lennard Books Ltd
Lennard House, 92 Hastings Street,
Luton, Beds LU1 5BH

Editor Michael Leitch
Design by Cooper·Wilson
Typeset by Goodfellow and Egan, Cambridge
Printed and bound in Spain by TONSA, San Sebastian

CONTENTS

INTRODUCTION
By Christopher Martin-Jenkins

One of the editorial decisions taken when *The Cricketer's* editorial office moved to Redhill in 1981 was to try to include in every issue of the magazine at least one article which would make people smile, if not laugh. Anyone who has been to our premises close to the station will know that neither the interior decorations nor the general area could be confused with a suite of offices in Park Lane and the editorial staff of, then, three, certainly needed some humour to get through each month without a call to the Samaritans, but that is beside the point. (In fact we all decided to stay in our damp little hovel a couple of years ago despite having a chance to move.) The real point was, of course, that cricket in the 1980s has become even more 'seriously' contested than ever it was. With big prize-money being put up by sponsors at the top, and littler sums being put up by sponsors at the bottom, giving, for example, village cricketers the chance to play at Lord's, there was, and still is, a danger that the fun of the game will be forgotten and many of its little nuances lost.

Of course it is a grave mistake to imagine that cricket was ever less than serious to those who play it, at any level, or to most of those who watch it. It *matters* whether England beat Australia or not; it *matters* whether Sheepstown beat Little Puddinghoe; it *matters* whether St Swithin's defeat Comberhome High; it even matters whether Ridley Garden City defeats Heseltine New Town. What is more, it matters to you, if you bat number four for any of these teams, whether you make four or 74; and there have been times during some of England's darker hours in recent years when it has seemed to matter even more to Ron Slogg of Littlegreen Wanderers than it has to the often-capped Wayne Paymemore of Worcester and England.

There are not many cricketers who really do not care who wins or how their own performance affects the winning or the losing. Dash it all, when Trevor Chappell, under instructions from brother Greg, committed the awful sin of bowling an underarm sneak to make sure the New Zealanders couldn't make six off the last ball to win a One-Day International, he was not even inventing anything new. Exactly the same thing had happened in different knockout competitions in Sussex and Surrey, the guilty clubs being suspended from the competition in both cases.

Some of cricket's most amusing moments come, in fact, because players are trying too hard. Not long ago, I was so eager to hit a portly purveyor of gently rolled leg-breaks over the long-on boundary, and so early with my attempted lofted on-drive, that I actually managed to lift the ball off the bottom of the bat into my own face. And I still recall, with an embarrassed blush, elegantly leaving another leg-break outside my off-stump, only to over-balance and be stumped, playing no stroke! The game can, and does, make fools of us all. The best story of many good ones in this anthology from *The Cricketer* is, I believe, the one told by Ian Peebles of Major-General R.M. Poore playing for MCC in the twilight of his career in a match in the West country. The picture conjured up of the General desperately revolving on his axis as he vainly tries to sight a skier under the wide periphery of his panama is hilarious – and not many writers have, like Peebles, the skill to make such a scene seem as funny on paper as it must have been at the time.

We need, therefore, to be able to laugh not just at ourselves but at cricket in general if we are to keep the game in proportion and not just to laugh, but to look at the game's diversions and by-ways, its eccentricities and eccentrics. This *The Cricketer* has been doing since its inception, long before the 1980s when, for a time, Peter Tinniswood produced perhaps the most irreverent writing the magazine has ever seen. Alas, it offended some readers but I hope a small sample here of life in Witney Scrotum will not dissuade anyone from sampling the remainder of a rich and varied selection of cricket's lighter side.

The game is seen herein from every angle, from characters on the Hill at Sydney where David Townsend's friend Annabelle observed that 'the crowd were with the Australians but some of the Australians should have been with the crowd', to the inside of a dressing-room with Mike Stevenson's team of eleven characters. He includes, I am glad to say, that extraordinary man R.J.O. Meyer, whom I saw one afternoon at Marlborough bowling literally every form of right-arm delivery – from fastish outswing with the new ball to under-arm leg-breaks with the old.

Another character adoringly portrayed here is Arthur Mailey, by R.C. Robertson-Glasgow, whose own engaging personality is graphically described by A.P. Singleton. We also include what must be some of the most sublime writing ever produced by that genius 'Crusoe', written in 1928 about his cricketing days with Oxford. Here is a taste of it:

Breathes there a man with a soul so dead, who, as he plays against Sussex at Brighton and bowls on that perfect wicket, has not thought of the palmy days of English batting, when Ranji's silk shirt fluttered in the breeze, and the bowler watched with a wondering dismay as his best and fastest sped, with a wizard glance, to the leg boundary; when Charles Fry's broad bat and iron back-play were waiting for you at the other end? They couldn't always get the other side out, I know; that would have ruined the Championship. They had no Tate then, bowling opening overs fit to make the gods weep tears of amber, to win the matches after those great ones had made defeat well-nigh impossible.

Good imaginative writing is not, however, Crusoe's sole preserve. You will find all sorts of pleasant surprises in this collection, even including what, to me at least, was a new F.S.T. anecdote:
'Come on Fred,' said the skipper (as one of England's greatest triers labours back for yet another over late on a hot day), 'England expects.'
'England's always expectin',' remarked Fred with a lifting of one dark eyebrow, 'that's why she's called the mother country.'
I was intrigued, too, by the county preview of 1922 in which 'Henry' discussed the season's prospects with three county captains – Tennyson of Hampshire, Calthorpe of Warwickshire and Fender of Surrey. All were confident of the Championship which, needless to say, Yorkshire actually went on to win. 'Henry' quoted an ingenious plan by Tennyson to have George Brown bowling and wicket-keeping at the same time in order to get rid of the alternative wicket-keeper, Livsey, and to include someone else who could bat better. But the curious irony is that in that very season Livsey made his famous 110 not out, sharing stands of 172 for the ninth wicket with Brown and 70 for the last with Boyes, to turn the match with Warwickshire on its head after Hampshire had been bowled out for 15 in the first innings.
Other gems ancient and modern to which I would particularly point the way include Peebles on Sydney Barnes; J.J. Warr on the day that Nobby Clarke swore vengeance; Peter Roebuck, when still in the ranks of Somerset, on a team-talk by the captain; Terry Wright on how county committees choose their overseas players; Bomber Wells on the character of pitches in various parts of the country – would their character was so consistent today; Mary Ann Smethers on the curse of cricket besotted sons as well as a cricket-mad husband; Henry Grierson on the now-

doomed ground at Hastings; Graham White discussing the true sound of leather on willow; and Geoffrey Morton proposing, but not naming, a modern bespectacled eleven. (How about this one from recent times – I have had to ask Geoff Howarth, a very occasional wicket-keeper, to take the gauntlets because I cannot think of any famous bespectacled 'keeper since R.A. Young and Paul Gibb):

Boycott, Greenidge, Zaheer Abbas, Clive Lloyd, M.J.K. Smith, E.J. Barlow, G.P. Howarth, Pringle, Allott, Hemmings and Doshi.

Not at their best on rainy days!

Cricket tours have always been a source of fun: Horace Brearley, Mike's father, writes on cricket in California; Ray Robinson describes what cricket tours used to be like off the field, BM (before Murdoch); and E.J. Metcalfe recalls the Free Foresters' tours of Ireland. They were strenuous work, as his daily timetable explains:

'Breakfast at 9, a round of golf; cricket from 11.30 to 6; lawn tennis till 8; dinner at 8.30; dancing till one.'

Life has changed much since that sort of tour was commonplace and it is no longer possible even to imagine that it cost only £140 to go on a three-month round trip to Australia in 1931–32 travelling first-class on the Orient Line. But other advertisements suggest that some things are not as new as we believe them to be. There, in June 1932, is a drawing of a Zodex water-absorbing roller which looks exactly like the ones buzzing up and down our Test grounds (albeit with a motor attached) in the late 1980s.

Even the future is not ignored in the lighter pages of *The Cricketer*. Peter Thompson imagined, in his '2003 – a Yorkshire Odyssey', a Yorkshire landscape pitted with the scars of the Civil War between forces pro and anti Geoff Boycott. But it was possible to take even that issue too seriously. Some years ago, when that particular matter unseated the entire Yorkshire committee and when Yorkshiremen could talk of little else, I attended the York District League dinner as a guest. As I sat down, the opening gambit of the committee-man next to me was:

'Well, my motion were passed by League committee – 19 for, 6 against.'

'Are you pro Boycott or anti?' I asked, innocently.

'Oh nay, nay,' he said disparagingly, '19 for apple pie tonight, only six for fruit salad and ice cream.'

SCHOOLDAYS

IT HAPPENED AT HASTINGS
By Henry Grierson

In the summer of 1907 that old cheat, Dame Fortune, favoured me with three donkey's nods as she passed on her way to make the rich richer. She hasn't troubled about me since, but let's get on with the nods. I was nearly sixteen (let me help you, I'm 77) and had just succeeded in oiling into the Bedford School XI – our worst side for years – and in addition to participating in a number of hidings, I had the honour of playing against three members of the touring South Africans, brought down in a scratch team by E.H.D. Sewell, the Surrey coach, and himself an Old Bedfordian. They were that fine opening bat, Louis Tancred, the elder Snooke (S.D.), and a grand hitter from the Transvaal named M.E. Smith, who held his bat very low down, as I noticed when the ball was being recovered from the River Ouse, or thereabouts, off my bowling. Unless *Wisden 1968* is at fault, which is doubtful, Smith is still around, aged 84, bless him. Needless to say, I defeated none of them, but getting into the School side was a decent first nod.

And then the summer holidays, with the joy of knowing that we were bound for Hastings, where I knew that there was a cricket Festival to look forward to, plus the possibility of schoolboy matches in that hotbed of sportsmanship. Thus I took my small cricket bag, as also did my buddy, Bertie Moran, who came with us, and who had his Second XI colours at Bedford.

Thus the next nod occurred two days after our arrival down south. Bertie and I were exploring the out-back of St Leonard's when, on a sudden, in the shade of an enormous gasometer, we observed a cricket net with men in a variety of kit at practice. We leaned on the five-barred gate overlooking the ground, and waited for manna to drop. It did, in the shape of a burly bloke in black boots. 'Do you boys play cricket?' 'Yes, sir,' said we, simultaneously, hoping that the gift of near Knighthood would further our cause. 'Then turn up tomorrow just before two. St Leonard's Gasworks, that's us, is two short, so we can do with you. We play Hastings Gasworks, and we want to lick 'em. What's yer nimes?' We told him. 'All right, Geeson and Moorhen, see you both tomorrer,' said the burly gasman, smiling kindly.

If you are an impulsive gasometer watcher, as I've been since 1907, you will know that the fat bit varies in height according to the amount of gas in the brute – Surrey members are, naturally, adept in the art. Thus, on our arrival at the ground it was apparent that the guys responsible for filling the tank had fallen down on the job, and only the supporting ironmongery was visible. We won the toss, and our big friend asked us where we batted, to which we modestly replied, 'Anywhere.' And lo, we were invited to open, with Bertie kindly giving me the strike, which I did not want. I took centre and waited; the delivery was a slow-medium full-toss on the leg side which was deposited slap bang in the middle of the gasometer, and never seen again. We ran four before someone shouted 'Lost ball', and when the general excitement and score had been adjusted it was found that no other ball was available. But, as you have already surmised, the position was stabilised by Geeson (big-hearted even in his youth) who produced one from his bag which he had won for taking six in an innings for Bedford (helped by three splendid lbw decisions by our umpire). We won the match; thus ended the second nod.

Jessop at Hastings
Now let us be fair; on the third occasion that the old lady bull had inclined her neck in my direction, I must record the fact that I sensed a slight relaxation of the usual steely glint, which I took as a good omen. And on looking at the local evening paper there it was – 'The following have been selected to play for the Gentlemen of the South against the Players of the South at the Central Cricket Ground, Hastings, starting tomorrow; Team: Mr G. L. Jessop,' etc., etc. I read no more, but rushed off to convey the tidings of great joy to Bertie Moran, seated on the hotel steps watching all the . . . watching all the . . . but to my astonishment he was doing nothing of the sort. He had a far-away look, full of longing and lack-lustre, and although he roused himself slightly when I told him the news and reminded him of that ferocious and remarkable century of Jessop's at the Oval in 1902 which shattered Australia, he remained unmoved. I asked what was biting him, and out it came. He couldn't accompany me to the match because he had decided to propose marriage: and it was the direct outcome of our helping to win the Gasworks

Ashes, no less. Permit me to explain. After our great victory we had been invited by the captain to join in the celebrations. We repaired to the Blue Bear Inn where, over a pint of shandy-gaff, Bertie had fallen head over pads in love with Bella, the buxom barmaid and red-head, with the beautiful big blue eyes, as they say.

As all boys (and most men) know, chaps in this state are beyond argument. Thus, next morning, I jumped on the horse-drawn tram alone, leaving Bertie to woo Bella. On arrival at the entrance gates my heart gave me a great bump as I heard a roar from the crowd, and a moment later the ball was crashing around the four-wheelers and hansom cabs awaiting fares. In I went and what a sight it was! Jessop had been batting for just over twenty minutes and his score was fifty-one. Seven men were on the boundary, but there was no stopping The Croucher. His driving was terrific all round the ground, and in addition he had a lovely late-cut, so that you needed at least sixteen men to arrest the torrent of runs. He reached his century with a fierce drive in *forty minutes*, and the crowd rose to the square-built England batsman. On he went, reaching 150 in just over *one hour*, finally getting himself out with his score at 191 made in ninety minutes. What a sight. I've seen a good deal of fine hitting in the sixty-one years that have intervened, but never its equal. When I got back to the hotel, still tingling with excitement, Bertie Moran was sitting on the steps. I told him what he had missed, and he nearly passed out. I asked him if he had been accepted, but he shook his head. 'Her red hair niffed a bit, so I chucked her. I've decided that girls are a waste of time – I'm sticking to cricket and Rugger in future, and I'll never marry.' But I never had the chance of checking up on this because, eight short years later he, and his beloved platoon of Indian soldiers, lay dead on the beaches of Gallipoli.

(Winter Annual, 1968–69)

WILL NO-ONE RID ME OF THIS TURBULENT GAME?
By Mary Ann Smethers

I cannot pretend that when I married my husband I did not know he liked cricket. I knew he had played two games each weekend for many years. I had become used to the numerous evening committee meetings and the cricket phone calls, frequent and lengthy, about fixtures, fund raising, catering, umpires, scorers, the state of the wicket, and, of course, the dreaded cry-offs. I'd lost count of the times I'd heard him pour oil over the troubled waters of selection. Injuries here, tantrums there, they all had to be sorted out. I'd even made the odd cricket tea until the supply of able and willing wives and girl friends dwindled to such an extent that, thankfully, outside caterers were brought in to do the job. I was quite happy to make lemon meringue pies for fund-raising discos and barbecues, and to watch a few games a season from the comfort of my deckchair.

After my sons were born everything changed. Taking two young children to a game of cricket was not restful. Keeping them the right side of the boundary line, off the sight screens and out of people's beer glasses was exhausting. Training them not to rush up to their father when he was out for a duck with loud inquiries as to his score was not easy. Still I kept taking them to games. It was nice to find a clean open space for them to play in, and both the boys and I enjoyed the company and a drink in the bar at the end of the game.

Little did I know what I was storing up for myself. Before I realised what was happening my eldest son, Tom, was hooked on the game. I suppose I should have seen the writing on the wall when at the age of two and a half he insisted on taking his cricket bat to bed with him. Photos of him, aged four, show him determinedly taking guard in front of the stumps he acquired for his birthday. Now he is seven, and it was this year that the full horror began to show itself.

"Perhaps if we all stopped trying to walk like Gary Sobers, some of us would get to school on time."

(1968)

Everything centres round cricket. Weekends last summer were eagerly anticipated. He studied the fixture list and the league table, and knew every player's highest score. He has already offered to help with selection next season. He practised bowling non-stop up and down the garden. Every morning I was given progress reports on how many overs he had bowled, and whether the ball was spinning, swinging, or just lost in the flower bed. He has a book on cricket statistics, which he walks to school reading in the morning and I have to prise out of his sleeping hand at night. When he is awake details of Test débuts, record-breaking stands, fastest centuries and bowling analyses trip off his tongue. He pointed out that our local greengrocer has the same initials as R. W. Marsh. There's hardly a player's middle name I do not know. When the Australians arrived he was in seventh heaven. He even managed to catch a virus for the First Test and was away from school. He lay on the sofa with a high temperature watching the game, lifting his head from the pillow to watch the replay every time a wicket fell.

No longer could I slumber in my deckchair at matches this summer. I was dragged out of it to bowl my John Embureys. I am not even spared when he does his homework. It was a week or two before I realised why learning his six times table caused him no difficulty: 15 overs an hour is ninety balls. Of course, nine times seven is easy because Allan Border scored it in the First Test, and Graham Dilley got seven times eight in the Third. He spends evening after evening writing out lists of real and imaginary games, played in such places as Georgetown and Madras. He spent many hours choosing his tour party to go to India. At 11 o'clock one night, fighting off sleep, he was wrestling with the problem of whether to send Wayne Larkins or Chris Tavaré. At seven o'clock the next morning there he was with an atlas in one hand and a sheaf of lists in the other, just asking me to check the location of the Indian Test grounds.

Sometimes I feel like screaming. If I hear another word about cricket I shall go crazy. To make matters worse I have just realised that the last photo I have of my second son, aged four, shows him determinedly taking guard in front of the stumps he acquired for his birthday. A state of near panic comes over me as I hear my eldest son explain to his brother about rhyming words. 'You know,' he says, 'words like Dilley, Willey, and Lillee.' A husband and two sons obsessed with cricket is more than anyone can bear.

(1982)

COLOURS
By F.E. Chapman

The following appears on the notice-boards of the school one morning in July:

'Smith major has gained his 1st XI colours.'

And there are probably very few, if any, happier persons in the world on that morning than Smith major. He knows that he is now, and henceforward, a marked man in his little world of school; that he, with one or two others, has gained a prize for which there has been such keen competition since the beginning of term; and that the 'pater' (who used to be a bit of a cricketer himself) will be delighted. Even Smith minor, his young brother, gains some reflected glory. Smith minor, according to all accounts, appears to be one of those lovable chaps who never can do anything right either in work or play, and makes the most amusing blunders.

A few days later comes the thrill of putting on the school blazer for the first time (it is probably of some self-colour, with a binding of some other colour, and the school crest on the pocket) and walking, somewhat self-consciously, down to the field among the plaudits of admiring comrades.

It is quite possible that Smith major, either from force of circumstances or from sheer mediocrity, will rise to no greater heights of fame in the world of cricket in later years. Yet the mere fact of his having been in his public school eleven will probably make him eligible to wear the colours of some reputable club if he wishes to do so. He may, on the other hand, have his chance, and be good enough, to aspire to a Blue, or a county cap. But in either case I don't believe that Smith major will feel a greater thrill than he felt on the morning in July when that notice appeared on the school boards that he had 'got his colours'.

I am not bold enough to make any comparison in the case of the man who gains his International colours, for such a thing is beyond my imagination.

And now let us suppose that our friend has got his Blue, may wear the colours of two or three well-known clubs (including the 'old school tie'), wants to get married, and has to work for his living. Will his decorations – or, in other words, his prowess on the cricket field – be of any use to him in the world of affairs? Will they help him to get a job in any other sphere than the teaching profession? Though I have had no personal experience in this respect, I should think not, or very little, unless he has some strong evidence of application and efficiency other than a striped tie. In fact, it may sometimes be a hindrance rather than a help. One can well imagine the head of a business firm saying to himself, 'This chap Smith seems a very nice fellow, but I'm afraid he is not accustomed to doing any steady, solid work: and, besides, he is sure to be constantly wanting time off to play some cricket match or other. I think I should be safer in offering the job to Williams.'

I remember well a noted cricketer of forty-odd years ago (it was R.P. Lewis, that wonderful wicket-keeper and equally futile bat) saying to me, 'When I got my Blue, I thought my fortune was made, but I soon found out my mistake; it was of no use whatever.'

Though I felt very loth to accept the sweeping statement contained in the last six words as literally true, it set me thinking. Is notoriety as a cricketer of no use whatever as a help to advancement? Setting aside all purely money-making pursuits, what about all 'the other professions in which men engage, the Army, the Navy, the Church, and the Stage'?

Surely in a cricket-loving country like ours, there must have been lots of cases in which, *ceteris paribus*, the scale has been turned in the cricketer's favour? Socially speaking, there can be no doubt that cricket prowess, however small, is of immense advantage, for it brings a man into

BEGGING THE QUESTION.

"You're out!"   "No, I ain't."
"Yes, you' are, you 'it the stumps."   "Well, it don't matter, I aint knocked 'em dahn."

(1921)

touch with people of all classes and sexes, whom he would otherwise have had no chance of meeting: and is not an enlarged circle of acquaintances a good thing from a business point of view?

I was once much amused by the remark of the 'local magnate' in a small Midland town concerning the curate, who, by the way, wore Crusader colours. 'We put up with his rotten sermons,' he said, 'because he has such jolly good shots on the leg-side!' Not much of an argument in the curate's favour, perhaps, but still,it shows that his cricket increased his congregation!

Smith major, however, is all right, for he has had sense enough to keep an eye on the future while at school and college, and being possessed (like all good cricketers) of a fair share of intelligence, has passed all his exams, creditably. A famous headmaster used to say that a man without brains never made a good cricketer. And so, S.M., aided perhaps by a certain amount of outside influence, gets a job without undue delay, and settles down to work for the income which will allow him to marry. But the pity of it is that henceforward he gets fewer and fewer chances of showing his colours on the playing area of the cricket grounds. The blazer, once so bright, gets more and more faded as the years roll by (does anybody over forty buy a new blazer?), and is at last consigned to the cupboard 'where the moth doth corrupt'.

But, thank goodness, the tie still remains, and will remain till his dying day to remind him and others that he once was young enough and was able to play cricket a bit. Is it childishness which prompts the old cricketer of eighty years or thereabouts to put on the colours of the club, or college, or regiment, or school, which at one time he was so proud to represent? Is it not rather a flicker of the flame of pardonable pride, enthusiam, and *esprit de corps*, which burnt so strongly forty, fifty, sixty years ago, when first he 'gained his colours'?

(1938)

THE FATHERS' MATCH
By David Melford

'It would be nice if the boys made about sixty,' said the Headmaster shaking the hand of the Fathers' captain. 'You may find that the umpires make some curious decisions if a shortfall looks likely.'

The Fathers' captain got the message and nodded. 'Fathers are allowed one pace run-up when bowling,' the Headmaster continued, 'we play twelve overs and when the boys have won the toss you will find that they will elect to bat first.'

He passed a coin to the captain of the School team who tossed it and said: 'You call, sir.' 'We'll bat,' he added, marginally before the coin hit the ground.

The Fathers gathered around their captain who had met only two of them previously over a medicinal gin and tonic when collecting offspring from birthday parties. 'Gentlemen,' he said, 'now is the time for modesty. Have any of you batted or bowled' – he looked around at them quickly – 'in the last fifteen years?'

No-one admitted to such an accomplishment and it was agreed that each should bowl at least one over. 'Would you take the first over?' said the Fathers' captain, addressing himself to the member of his team who happened to be holding the ball.

The Fathers distributed themselves evenly over the field and the first was bowled. 'Wide,' shouted the umpire and the school had opened their score.

Long hop
The next ball – a long hop craftily delivered outside the leg stump – drew the opening batsman down the wicket. He failed to make contact and the wicket-keeper removed the bails, inquiring, as he did so, how the umpire thought it was. The umpire gazed at the low clouds which a cold northerly wind was driving across the sky and the match continued. The third ball was well swept for four runs and the fourth nudged deftly past extra cover for two. The score mounted. Wickets began to fall.

The Fathers' captain was pre-occupied by selecting his next bowler on the basis of giving him the opportunity to bowl at his own son. Distracted by these calculations he returned the ball hard to the wicket-keeper, noticing only after it had left his hand that both batsmen appeared temporarily to have arrived at that end. Two overthrows were run. The School cheered.

At 36 for six the Headmaster remarked loudly that he would be surprised if any more catches were held and unaccountably none were. The twelve appointed overs passed with still three wickets to fall. 'All the boys should have a knock, I think,' said the Headmaster.

At 67 the last man was clean bowled and the School's innings came to an end. The Fathers captain was then called upon to decide his batting order. He had given some thought to the resolution of this delicate problem. 'Alphabetical,' he said promptly.

The Headmaster came over with the bats kindly provided by the school for the Fathers' use. These had been shaved on each side to a maximum width of 1½ins. 'Should the scores approach parity,' he remarked gravely, 'the other umpire and I will consult about the appalling light.'

prep school match

"Couldn't you have said good-bye to him at tea time, Mrs. Cuthbertson. We've already lost a lot of time through rain."

"Never mind the lofted pull, we'll have Nicholson in from the mid-wicket boundary."

"Don't overdo the backing-up, Parkinson."

"You'll have to bowl straighter before you warrant such an elaborate leg-trap, Prentice."

(Spring Annual, 1969)

Armed with these flimsy weapons, the Fathers' opening pair walked out to the accompaniment of sympathetic applause, The School team, whose fixture-list disrupted by the weather had involved them in a match each day for the past fortnight, were nothing if not in practice. Their fast bowler measured out his lengthy run with all the menace of the Fordendon blacksmith. The Fathers' opening batsman, preparing to face him, wished the drizzle would stop smearing his glasses.

In something under 15 minutes the Fathers were nine for five and honour was imperilled. The Headmaster glanced at the score board. 'No ball,' he shouted helpfully as the stumps were spreadeagled for the sixth time. The Fathers' captain glanced gratefully at him, painfully aware that a captain's innings in this situation would certainly be held to consist of more than two. Swinging hopefully at the next ball, he hit it over the square-leg boundary for six.

Ten runs later he called for a run on the assumption (a) that the fielder would misfield, (b) that, even if he didn't, the wicket-keeper would fail to collect the return, and (c) that he was pretty fast when running between wickets anyway. Mistaken on all counts, he was comprehensively run out.

Back in the pavilion, opinion among the Fathers was divided on whether their tail would wag hard enough to avoid humiliation. The Fathers' captain, wishing to advise his remaining men on the way the pitch was playing, discovered to his surprise that they were one man short. They had, indeed, only fielded 10 men, a fact which seemed to have escaped everyone's notice until now. Filled with sudden suspicion, he checked the list the Headmaster had given him to reassure himself there were 11 names on it.

He was saved from the dilemma of deciding who should bat twice by the School's twelfth man, a diminutive boy who arrived breathless, with impeccable timing, to announce that he was Perkins, Sir, and could he be substitute.

'Run,' he cried

His offer gratefully accepted, the boy was accoutred with haste to find that his services were required immediately at the non-striking end, 'Run,' he shouted shrilly – anxious to secure the strike – as the next ball flew off the batsman's pads down towards third man. The batsman, slightly hard of hearing at high frequencies, was gazing curiously after the ball and viewed with some surpise the arrival of the substitute in the crease beside him. The ball, meanwhile, had arrived back with the bowler who raised his arm to shatter the stumps, only to find the umpire standing firmly in front of them.

The substitute scuttled back to his crease just as the bowler circumvented the obstruction and removed the bails. 'Not quite quick enough,' said the umpire. 'Over.'

Three balls later the last of the Fathers was clean bowled, the total standing at sixty. The School won by seven runs.

'A fair result I think,' said the Headmaster, 'thank you all for turning out.'

'Three cheers for the Fathers,' said the School captain and – after these had been given and returned – 'Thanks for the match, Dad,' he added.

(1980)

THOUGHTS IN SPRING

LETTER FROM WITNEY SCROTUM
By Peter Tinniswood

Here in the heart of the glorious English countryside at Witney Scrotum we await the arrival of spring with breathless anticipation. It is only July yet already there are faint signs that Mother Nature is waking from her long winter sojourn.

Our bird-watching expert, Miss Roebuck from the dog biscuit shop, reports the first sighting of summer migrants on the water meadows at Cowdrey's Bottom. Garner's long-legged stilt. Hadlee's pimple-browed warbler, Richards's lissome boundary stalker – what a welcome addition they make to our drab and timid native fauna.

Although the snow still clings to the soaring buttresses of the summit of the massive Botham's Gut, and although the bitter north wind scours the valley bottom by Dredge's Elbow, we feel that spring cannot be too far away. If we look hard enough we can see hints that the season is about to break. Derek Randall, blinking in the shy, rain-soaked sunshine, has already emerged from his long winter hibernation spent in the darkest depths of his cricket bag buried at the bottom of his bedroom.

Our beloved Don 'Sir Oswald' Mosey, leader of the BBC Blackshirt Brigade, is drilling his commentary team in the claret repository at the rear of the Baxter Arms. And new shy green growth has appeared on old Squire Brearley's moleskin typewriter cover. But I am still wary. Not a clout shall I cast ere July be out.

I still cling steadfastly to my thermal plus fours and my waterproof spats, and the lady wife, wisely in my opinion, is still wearing her Barbour coat during midnight excursions on the ablutions front. Yes, for lovers of the 'summer game' the weather is a constant worry. It drove our groundsman to drink, loose women, and ghastliest of all by far, reading

FAMILY OF BRITISH MAMMALS DURING HIBERNATION.

(Spring Annual, 1958)

the unexpurgated autobiographies of Sir Geoffrey Boycott, most of them written by the great man himself.

Our present temporary groundsman, the village blacksmith and honorary toad cirumciser, Gooch, is, however, quietly confident that the square will be ready for action come the last two weeks of August. So I suppose we can't complain. With fortitude, good humour and typical English steadfastness let us face up to the worst the weather man throws at us during the coming months.

Let us remember that there is always someone in the world worse off than us – Good God, the weather's been so bad in Yorkshire that Ray Illingworth hasn't been able to get out for his old-age pension for six successive weeks. No wonder his Thermogene mittens are beginning to 'niff' a bit.

(1983)

TOCK . . . OR WHAT?
By Graham White

'Nothing,' I wrote, 'is more thrilling to the true cricketer's ear than the sweet "tock" of willow against leather.' And stopped.

I realise now that I shouldn't have stopped; I should have continued to hammer those typewriter keys till the page lengthened and the sentence disappeared from sight. But I have a passion for verbal accuracy – and I stopped.

'Tock,' I said aloud, and listened intently to the sound of it. Or was it 'plock'? Both words have been used by masters of cricket prose and either should have been good enough for me. Yet I hesitated.

'Tock,' I repeated. Then I tried 'plock' again. Were either of them precisely right or was it something in between? 'Twock,' for instance? I strove desperately to take my ears back to Lord's for a moment or two. Hammond – was he a tocker, a plocker or a twocker?

In the end I clapped the cover over the typewriter and strolled round to the cricket ground. It was Wednesday, and not the best day for research into the music of the game, for on Wednesdays the Kreislers and Menuhins of Wembury Park are seldom on show. Rather are they the occasions when first reserves for the third team find themselves opening the innings, and old gentlemen, long since retired, are pressed into reluctant service; and return ten minutes later with perfectly creased flannels, dazzling boots and suspiciously well-oiled bats.

Two stalwarts, Bill Masters and Jim Harding were at the wickets when I reached the pavilion, however, and as both were well set they suited my purpose admirably. Note book at the ready and pencil poised, I waited for the bowler to run up and jotted down the onomatopoeic results of the next six balls. And here they are:

'Wonk!' 'Wop!' 'Swapp!' 'Swonk!' 'Swop!' 'Twank!'

The field changed over, and Bill Masters, patient and obdurate, played an over as follows:

'Bap!' 'Bonk!' 'Bem!' 'Ponk!' 'Twack!' 'Bung!'

Yes, quite definitely, 'Bung!' But perhaps I should have mentioned before that Masters is left-handed.

I stayed on to the end of the innings, patiently listening for just one authentic, traditional 'Tock!' Curiously enough, it came from Simpson's bat, and Simpson bats number eleven.

'That shot of yours through the covers – the one that left third man standing,' I queried when he came out. 'Did you notice the sound it made?'

'I did,' said Simpson, cheerfully. 'Funny, wasn't it? Came off the back of the bat as a matter of fact.'

That evening I opened my notebook, inserted a new sheet of paper in the typewriter, and started afresh.

'Nothing,' I wrote, 'is more thrilling to the true cricketer's ear than the sweet "swonk!"' . . .'

And stopped. Sweet 'bonk?' . . . Sweet 'ponk'?

And sighed long and deep. And arrived at the conclusion that it is neither 'tock', 'chock', 'plock', nor any other specific sound. A cricket bat has almost as many notes as a Stradivarius, and most of them are sweet to the ear. Of the batsman, at any rate.

I exclude my own bat, of course. How simple would be the writer's job if all bats were like mine. Possibly, it is unique. At all events I know of no other bat which, Saturday after Saturday and season after season produces the same unchanging note which is at once the bowler's delight and the fieldsman's heaven-sent opportunity.

'Snick!!'

(1946)

CRICKET FEVER
By A Cornishman

As hay fever is associated with the time of the ripening corn and mown grass, so cricket fever comes with the primroses, violets and celandines of the spring, and when the first daisy shows its cheerful white face on the lawn. The March sun warms the bones, and a sense of invigoration sends

THE FITNESS OF THINGS

This is the time of the year when hordes of muscular young devotees of "THE GAME" strenuously prepare for the approaching season, using approved and recognised methods of the M.C.C.C. (MUSCLE CULTURE (CRICKET) COMMITTEE) some of which are shown here. Though the knees-bend exercises for stumpers and finger raising and lowering for umpires are excluded.

But very soon they will be their happy, carefree, fit selves once more when conditioned by the old fashioned field punishment drill.

(Spring Annual, 1959)

every cricketer burrowing into the cupboards where the bat, ball and stumps have been hibernating while the battered rugby ball and muddied jersey have been taking precedence.

You feel you just cannot wait, and the bat is caressed and oiled, and the ball polished endlessly on the seat of the trousers in between vicious leaps and imaginary deliveries from a bowling crease on the drawing room carpet. Deadly new grips are tried to produce the unplayable fast leg-break or the very late away-swinger, and the batting practice usually accounts for several pieces of furniture, terminating abruptly when the lampshade representing, of course, a fast, rising ball from Lindwall is hooked for six into the fireplace, whence, as a very chastened deep square-leg, you retrieve it with dustpan and brush under the eyes of a furious mother. However she is soon placated when you lay the table for her, and help with the washing up without the usual moaning, and possibly she even takes a little fielding practice with you afterwards.

This, then, is how the fever attacks most of us, but in Cornwall it may be recognised by several additional symptoms, the first of these being the whist drive in aid of the club just before Christmas. Prizes are provided by the local cricketing farmers, and vary from a turkey for the winner, through every conceivable form of poultry down to a dozen eggs for the booby prize. With the proceeds the field is rented, and the cows and other farmyard matter shortly afterwards evicted. Then it is that the peculiar complication of 'mole cidal mania' breaks out in me, and whatever the weather I spend early morning and late afternoon furiously excavating with my spade, trying to find the main runs of the wretched animals that are doing their best to provide a bowlers' paradise at the Cow Shed end. My parents become alarmed at this outbreak too, when the skins of the slain appear pinned to boards leaning against the walls of the drawing room, which, with its constant fire, is the only place which prevents them turning mildewy. As the moles decrease, so the malady cures, until it seems completely cured by the time of the Calcutta Cup match at Twickenham.

Repairing their nets
The relapse occurs when the whole village eventually emerges from hibernation, and the fishermen begin caulking, painting, and rigging their boats, drawn high up the slipway out of reach of the winter gales, repairing their nets, and tying lines and weights onto the new, green, wicker lobster pots. The young ravens will soon be hatching under Pen-y-Vaden point, where the starry, white flowers of the wild narcissus are gently blown by the light breeze, which sends the sea dancing away in the sunlight towards distant Gull Rock. Spring is everywhere, and when

BEFORE AND AFTER

the day's work is done the cricketers gather on the pitch, and soon many willing hands are dragging the heavy roller to and fro over the rapidly flattening square, while the out-field receives its initial scytheing.

The conversation is entirely of cricket; sometimes the prospects of the coming season are discussed with unbounding optimism; sometimes the victories of last year are recalled, with the many fighting innings and the great bowling feats, such as Fred's eight wickets for 2 runs, taken in the gathering dusk of an August evening when the War Ag were dismissed for 12, eight of which were byes which sneaked past the wicket-keeper in the gloom. Then there is the never ending discussion of Past v Present or Hobbs v Compton, but soon we can stand it no more, and when the quota of rolling for the day is over, a bat and several balls appear as if by magic. A couple of sticks are broken from the hedge, and Arnold, the captain, hangs his coat on these at the side of the square to represent the wicket, which he proceeds to defend vigorously against anything we offer him. Arms are stiff and length is bad, but the will is there and the pitch does the rest, and it is never long before a creeper lodges up against the bottom of the coat and it is time for another batsman to loosen up.

Old 'Erb is always there behind the wicket, chuckling through his tobacco-stained whiskers, and clad in the usual decrepit pair of breeches and mud-encrusted boots, flailing at anything which eludes the batsman with a venomous looking pitchfork. A number of nippers chase around the outfield, mainly in the direction of long-on where the majority of balls are despatched in truly agricultural fashion, and when their elders become tired and thirsty and wend their way back to the 'Plume', they bowl themselves, each trying to out-do the other in speed and ferocity.

All too soon twilight comes, and Bill collects the bat and balls, and with a cheery 'See you tomorrow,' wanders off along the path to his shop overlooking the port. The blackbirds have joined in their evening concert as I slowly wander home and leave the field to buzzards, soaring on motionless wings on the upper currents of air, round and round against the delicate pinks and greys of the sunset. I hear the wild bubbling calls of the curlew flighting along the creek as I enter the house, and they seem to complete my contentment, and inspire this, the latest complication of a malady for which, happily, there is no cure.

(Spring Annual, 1950)

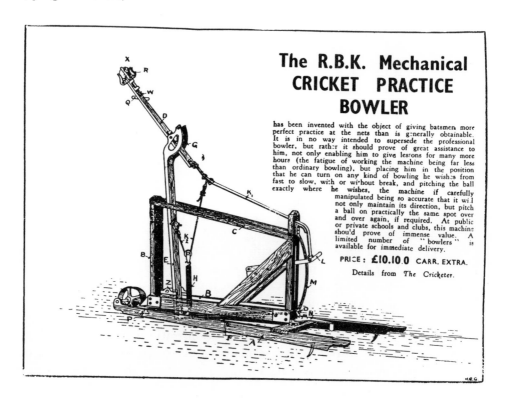

The R.B.K. Mechanical CRICKET PRACTICE BOWLER has been invented with the object of giving batsmen more perfect practice at the nets than is generally obtainable. It is in no way intended to supersede the professional bowler, but rather it should prove of great assistance to him, not only enabling him to give lessons for many more hours (the fatigue of working the machine being far less than ordinary bowling), but placing him in the position that he can turn on any kind of bowling he wishes from fast to slow, with or without break, and pitching the ball exactly where he wishes, the machine if carefully manipulated being so accurate that it will not only maintain its direction, but pitch a ball on practically the same spot over and over again, if required. At public or private schools and clubs, this machine should prove of immense value. A limited number of "bowlers" is available for immediate delivery.

PRICE: £10.10.0 CARR. EXTRA.

Details from *The Cricketer*.

CRICKET WATCHING

THE SELECTION COMMITTEE
By C.C.

I had not been on the car five minutes before I discovered that their names were Joe, Jim and Albert, and that their conversation was far more interesting than my book. For they were solving the problem that will soon be giving Messrs Warner, Perrin, Gilligan, Hobbs and Rhodes some thoughtful moments.

'Well, my team would be,' said Albert, with a judicial air, ticking them off on his fingers, ''Obbs, Sutcliffe, 'Allows, 'Endren, Woolley . . .'

'Dunno so much about Woolley,' interrupted Jim.

'Why, what's wrong with him?'

'Oh, there ain't nothing exactly wrong with 'im,' Jim replied. 'But what about A.P.F. Chapman?'

Albert's face assumed an expression of indescribable disgust. 'A blinking amateur!' was his scathing retort.

Jim reddened, as a Labour leader might redden if caught lunching with a lord. But he stuck to his point. 'And why not an amateur?' he demanded aggressively. 'They're human beings, ain't they?' he continued, as though propounding some astonishing, but undeniable truth.

Albert, however, was adamant. 'You've got to have one amateur as captain – that's bad enough. Anyway,' he continued, resuming his selection, 'my team would be 'Obbs, Sutcliffe, 'Allows, 'Endren, Woolley, Carr, Kilner, Tate, Root, Macaulay and Strudwick.'

Jim remained unmoved. 'And you call that a team!' he exclaimed, slowly, and with emphasis.

'Well, and what's wrong with it?' Albert flared. 'You can't pick a better one!'

'Ho, can't I! Why, my ole woman could pick a better team than that with 'er eyes shut and a pin!'

This, I felt, was a distinct point to Jim. But Albert was not to be shaken. He stood by his selection and defied Jim to better it. Jim was nothing loth.

'I'd have 'Earne instead of 'Allows,' he said, 'Fender instead of Carr, Chapman insead of Woolley, Jupp instead of Root, and Duckworth for Struddy. And if they couldn't beat the Australians I don't know who could! What do you say, Joe?'

Joe was considerably older than the others. Thus appealed to, he broke a ruminative silence: 'What I says is – we wants another Georgie 'Irst.'

Albert was getting annoyed. 'Anyone'd think as 'Irst was the only blinking cricketer what ever lived, the way you go on about 'im!' he exclaimed.

'If only we 'ad George 'Irst,' Joe continued, with the didactic emphasis of his type, 'we'd . . .'

'Oh, blow Hirst!' cried Albert. 'What I want to know is: would any sane man give 'Earne another . . .'

'Let the old 'un have 'is say,' Jim broke in, catching at the chance of gaining an ally. ''E knows more about cricket than you do, anyway!'

This, to Albert, was the final insult. ''Oo does?' he demanded, with an aggressive thrust of the chin.

''E does!'

'Ho, does 'e! An' I suppose,' Albert grew heavily sarcastic, 'you'll be saying you do next.'

'Well, an' p'r'aps I do!'

'P'r'aps you do not!' Albert answered. 'Why, I bet you ain't even seen a Test match!'

'I never said I 'ad, did I? And I bet you ain't, neither!'

'Well, an' what if I ain't?'

The voice of the conductor caused an unwelcome interruption, but all the way down the car steps the discussion continued.

And as the bell clanged, and the tram moved on, a querulous voice came floating upwards:

'If only we 'ad Georgie 'Irst!'

(1926)

THE CORNET WORRIED GEORGE GUNN MORE THAN THE BOWLING . . .
By Neville Cardus

Mr Dennis Morris, the MCC Publicity Officer, has an idea that crowds at cricket matches might like to hear music played during lunch or tea intervals, or any other periods of interruption to the day's major procedure. Conceivably I might be of some help here – suggesting the music most likely to suit a particular player or situation. For example, at the beginning of an England XI innings, after Milburn has been dismissed, selections from Bellini's 'La Somnambula' would surely enchant the drowsy ear and scene. 'O ruddier than the cherry' is a song

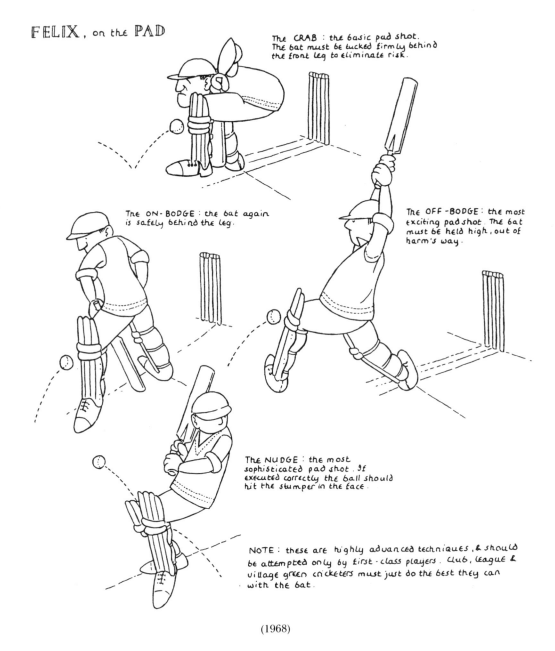

FELIX, on the PAD

The CRAB : the basic pad shot. The bat must be tucked firmly behind the front leg to eliminate risk.

The ON-BODGE : the bat again is safely behind the leg.

The OFF-BODGE: the most exciting pad shot. The bat must be held high, out of harm's way.

The NUDGE : the most sophisticated pad shot. If executed correctly the ball should hit the stumper in the face.

NOTE : these are highly advanced techniques, & should be attempted only by first-class players. Club, league & village green cricketers must just do the best they can with the bat.

(1968)

which any seamer might instinctively sing, as he polished the new ball; and I have known several occasions when and where Elgar's 'Enigma' variations would have been entirely in tune with an innings of Colin Cowdrey.

Music accompanying actual play at cricket is of course, no new thing – we have heard it for years at Canterbury. But it isn't a generally known fact that once upon a time a band dispersed music during battle in Test matches at Sydney – at any rate, dear old George Gunn assured me that a military band was very much in action when, in December 1907, he scored a century for England v Australia at Sydney.

'I went in to bat first wicket down, and soon we'd lost two wickets for next to nothin'. Then after lunch, when I'd made about 30, band started.' (George, by the way, was quite a good pianist. He played, as he batted, 'by ear'.) 'Well,' he continued, 'I could hardly settle down after lunch, because cornet was out of tune. They were playin' selections from "Mikado", and cornet was never right. It bothered me all afternoon, I couldn't concentrate. And Hanson Carter, Australian wicket-keeper, you know, said to me, "George, that cornet seems to be givin' you more worry than our bowling."'

Gunn, his ear distracted by the cornet, scored 119. But, as he more than once pointed out to me, 'Batsmen make the mistake of taking too much notice of the bowling.' Frankly, I myself have no wish to hear music while good cricket is going on – an innings by Graveney is cricket's own music itself. Still, I can appreciate Mr Morris's desire to provide us with ameliorative distractions, especially on an average day of county cricket. He might introduce side-shows – say, television screens showing *real* live sport in progress at Wimbledon, in overseas soccer, or from Ascot.

(1967)

A LETTER FROM ANNABELLE . . .
By David Townsend

Sydney, February 1987
Dear Mum,

Guess what? My new boyfriend Greg took me to see England play Australia at the Sydney Cricket Ground last month.

It wasn't what Daddy would call a real game – like the time he took us all to Canterbury for the day and you fell asleep – it was a one-day international. Not only that, but a day/night game as well!

Australians love this sort of cricket. An hour before the start the ground was packed with men in vests carrying cases of beer, accompanied by their wives and girlfriends in colourful shorts and bikinis. There was a real carnival atmosphere.

Greg tried to get us into one of the big new stands, but all the tickets had been sold months ago. That left us with only one option – to sit on the notorious Sydney Hill.

Greg says the Hill isn't as large as it used to be, but it still has a fearsome reputation. He explained that as an English person I would be wise not to give away my allegiance by saying too much. At least, I think that's what he meant by, 'Keep yer Pommie mouth shut'.

We found a little patch of grass towards the back and laid out our blanket. Greg's two friends, Greg and Greg, unloaded our beer and began to 'get into it' as they say out here. On the field various people were examining the pitch. A large girl in a patterned dress adjusted the dials on an impressive looking machine and then a tall, balding man pointed at them as he spoke into a camera. Behind and above us, a gigantic scoreboard made up of thousands of tiny lights belted out an advertisement for Coca-Cola as the two captains tossed up.

Australia batted first. As their two openers appeared in their bright green and yellow kit the whole ground seemed to sprout wildly waving flags. A thought struck me that it must have been an Englishman who awarded Australia the national colours of envy and cowardice, but I didn't say anything.

The English team looked far more stylish in their two shades of blue. The crowd around us were very loud and not too polite with their language. When one chap hovered in front of us, Greg's friend Greg told him, in no uncertain terms, to 'Sit down yer mug'. When his request was ignored he repeated it – still without response. Finally, he suggested, 'Well at least stand sideways, and we'll watch through yer ears!' I thought that was tremendously funny.

There were thunderous cheers whenever the Australians hit fours, and loud booing if the English fielders dared get in the way. When Ian Botham came on to bowl, the entire Hill burst into a chorus of 'Botham is a Junkie'. Secretly though, I'm sure most of them wish he was Australian – some of the girls were singing 'Botham is a Hunkie'.

Greg's other friend Greg tells me he has never seen the end of a one-day match. He has been four times, but left early on each occasion. Greg explains this is because he was arrested twice and escorted out twice. As the afternoon wears on and the cans disappear it's easy to see why.

The 'dinner break' between the two innings lasts for nearly an hour. I suppose if you are sitting in the Members this gives you time to do just about anything, but we couldn't forsake our little piece of the Hill, and the wait became very uncomfortable. We were entertained while we waited with an exhibition of American football. In the setting it seemed very appropriate and Greg bought us all a hamburger and Coke. The lights were switched on for the start of the English innings and lit up the ground like six candles on a birthday cake.

You may think I was the only English person brave enough to sit on the Hill, but no! Down below us a group of boys huddled around a banner that read 'DHSS WORLD TOUR 86/87'. They looked like the sort of people Daddy is always complaining about having to pay his taxes to keep. They did seem very poor though – all four of them were sharing the same cigarette. As the smoke drifted up towards us, Greg's friend Greg said: 'Botham's on the Hill'. Everyone laughed, but I didn't see him anywhere.

The night drew in and the lights got brighter. I suddenly realised why they call it Kerry Packer's Circus – all the players look like clowns with their fancy dress and painted lips. Allan Border with his sad face looks particularly clownlike – all he needs to complete the image is a red nose and a bobble on his hat. Greg says that Greg Matthews even plays like a clown. Any mention of Australia's champion all-rounder sparks off a furious debate. Is Matthews better than Botham, not as good as Geoff Miller, or simply the finest disco dancer ever to have played in the Birmingham League?

The argument only ended when Matthews and Botham came face to face in the middle. I think Botham came out on top, but I'm not sure because most of my energies at this point were directed towards stopping Greg's other friend Greg from hurling cans at the English group in front of us. I was determined he would see the end of this game.

Fights, police charges and arrests were going on all around us. Two portly men in underpants ran onto the field despite repeated warnings over the loudspeaker system that anyone doing so would be arrested (running onto the field, nothing about underpants!). The police always had the upper hand, but on the field the boys in blue were struggling. When England needed 18 to win off the final over, Greg and his friends were prematurely celebrating.

Allan Lamb spoiled their fun – and Greg's other friend Greg's chances of seeing the end of a game – by hitting a huge six which landed on Greg's head rendering him unconscious. England won with a ball to spare. The Hill filed away in a subdued, if not sober manner. Greg summed the match up by saying, 'The crowd were with the Australians, but some of the Australians should have been with the crowd.'

It was nothing like Canterbury.

Love, Annabelle x x

(1987)

Test-pieces

Rays

A light-hearted look at some possible effects of the Australian's tour this coming summer.

"You don't have to take it out on me—
I didn't choose them!"

"I don't think I'll ask him if he can come just at
the moment, mother—England are following on!"

"You would have to get out just as things are critical!"

"Just because I don't know exactly how many
goals the Australians have scored this tour you
think I know nothing about the game."

"Hurry up and decide—
they're coming out."

EPISODE AT LORD'S
By C.I. Thornton

There are always funny and interesting things happening at cricket. I can remember one or two that amused me very much at the time – one in particular, I think, about 1865 when I was at Eton. My tutor, the Rev. G.R. Dupuis, one of the best, took one or two boys up to Lord's to see Gents v Players. Anyhow, W.G. and E.M. Grace were playing. In those days they used to lunch at one long table, in the old Pavilion, of course. I had the good fortune to sit close to 'W.G.' and 'E.M.', whom I naturally worshipped, never having seem them before. Well, the first thing 'E.M.' did was to take his boots off – they were side-spring ones – saying to 'W.G.', 'Oh, my feet are so dooced sore,' and put them under his chair. I though what a funny performance, as I had never seen it done at Eton. 'E.M.' then sat down at the head of the table, and sent for some cold beef, which duly arrived. He then asked for some salad, of which he took a liberal help, covering the cold beef entirely. When he wasn't looking, the waiter came up and took away his plate, thinking it was the salad dish. 'What are you doing with my plate?' said 'E. M.', 'I ain't begun yet.' 'Pardon,' said the waiter, 'I thought it was the salad dish.' He and I became great friends, as he used to come down to Canterbury during the week. His book is a most interesting one, and shows how thoroughly his heart was in the game.

(1927)

HUTTON À LA FRANÇAISE
By Cdr H. Emmet, RN (retd)

'Ce garçon là,' said my neighbour, gesturing in the direction of Hutton, 'vous me dites qu'il est un cricketeur du premier ordre?' 'Mais certainement,' I replied firmly. 'Tiens!' He moved his head slowly from side to side, the corners of his mouth turned down deprecatingly. Nobody but the French can so effectively express disbelief without actually putting it into words. I felt embarrassed. The man sitting next to me had purposely delayed his return to Paris to satisfy his curiosity about this mad English addiction to *le cricket*. And here he was, already as good as criticising Hutton. If, when he first arrived, he had been puzzled by the eccentric formalities of starting a game of cricket, it was nothing to the deep mystification which visibly developed in him as he absorbed the answers to a fusillade of questions to which he subjected me. Clearly, the English were even madder than he had thought.

There were all the usual ones about the technicalities of batting, bowling, scoring runs, overs (*how on earth do you translate that?*), maidens (*vierges?*), fielders and ways of getting out. The duration of the match was a major issue. This one, a Test match, was allotted four days of six hours each. *Incroyable!* Why did people come to watch if they couldn't see the finish? I was ready for that one. The Tour de France, I pointed out, extended over three weeks!

I judged it prudent to divert the discussion into less contentious channels by enlarging on the aesthetics of cricket and its surroundings. Thank goodness, I thought, we were at Lord's and not The Oval. All the same, my neighbour appeared profoundly unconvinced.

It was inevitable that the conversation should turn to personalities. As Hutton was batting, what more suitable than to treat my friend to a little eulogy on the master of contemporary England batsmen with, of course, a reference to his 364 against Australia.

'Trois cent soixante-quatre?' Amazing! He glanced at the scoreboard. Hutton had been batting an hour and had scored six. I knew what the next question would be, and sure enough it came. No, it had *not* taken him sixty and two-thirds hours.

The question that followed soon after was also predictable, for it was now one o'clock. At what hour does one lunch and for how long? My answer only added to his general astonishment, this time mingled with horror. Forty minutes? Only forty minutes for lunch? So the English were even so barbaric as to sacrifice the most precious hours of the day, to put up with queueing, discomfort and near-starvation, all for the sake of these tribal rites.

He stood up, raised his hat and held out his hand. I would understand, he said, that a Frenchman was accustomed to something a little different. But he would be back later to see whether this "Utton is going to mark trois cent soixante-quatre.'

He duly reappeared at 2.30, obviously brimming with virtue at having curtailed his lunch to a mere hour and a half. 'Alors,' he greeted me, 'qu'est-ce qu'il fait ce 'Utton?' I pointed to the board which showed that he had now reached 18 but refrained from mentioning that it had taken nearly two hours. This would only have led to further exasperating statistical exercises.

Later, I announced that we had a real treat in store, with Edrich and Compton, England's most brilliant and attractive batsmen, operating in tandem. My Frenchman patently felt he had heard all this before, and that this was where he had come in for he sighed deeply and rose to his feet. He regretted that he was obliged to save himself (all right in French, but a little ambiguous in English) as he had to catch his train.

And so we parted, and I could settle down to revel undistracted in the Middlesex pair as they carved the South African bowlers to all parts of the field.

It did not matter so much then, that a Frenchman had missed seeing Edrich and Compton. What did matter, as things turned out, was that it was the only time I ever saw Hutton bat.

(1963)

A CONVERSATION AT LORD'S
By Ben Travers

Note: The Characters in this brief summary of the day's play are familiar but entirely fictitious. They occupy an otherwise carefully avoided corner of Lord's Pavilion and they are:

Mr Dodo Doornail (aged 92).
Mr Jonah Glump (aged 70, a very late Indian Civil Servant).
Mr Malcolm Puter (a somewhat younger enthusiast).
Mr Masterman Nowall (a still younger enthusiast).

Glump: Very slow, these fellers.
Doornail: M'mph. Put me in mind of Bannerman.
Glump: Eight runs in half an hour.
Doornail: Or Arthur Shrewsbury.
Nowall: Ah, well, sir – start of an innings . . .
Puter: Yes and a bit green on top . . .
Nowall: Doing quite a bit in the air too . . .
Puter: Using the seam; concentrating on out-swingers . . .
Glump: Why the devil can't they bowl on the wicket? That's what it's there for, isn't it?
Puter: Actually, I agree. This fellow bowled one on the wicket two overs ago and he induced a top thick outside edge to gully.
Glump: Edge? He's got a whole damn bat. What's he want to use the edge for? Doesn't he know this new law – only gets sixty-five overs in the first innings?
Nowall: Not now. They scrapped that long ago.
Glump: Oh, did they? Then I suppose they'll plod along to try and get points for first innings lead.
Puter: No, no; they scrapped that too.
Doornail: W.G. was a good point. I saw him catch Harry Trott there off Tom Richardson. No, Lohmann.
Glump: Well, what's stopping 'em making some runs?

How to play TEST CRICKET №1 Batting.

PRODDING   NODDING   SLOGGING

SNICKING   MISSING

OR MERELY ACKNOWLEDGING THE APPLAUSE FOR A CENTURY

(1974)

Nowall: We've told you, sir. They must see the shine off the seamers.

Doornail: No; come to think of it, it was Lockwood.

Puter: Hallo, that was a good delivery. Nearly rattled his furniture. That struck me as a cutter.

Glump: What d'you mean, a cutter. If only this batsman was a cutter . . .

Doornail: William Gunn was a good cutter.

Glump: Another no-ball. Why do they keep bowling no-balls?

Puter: Dragging the popping-crease. There's a rule against that now.

Nowall: Or the bowling crease.

Puter: Not instead of.

Nowall: Both.

Puter: Either.

Nowall: As well as. Damn good, these new rules.

(*pause*)

Puter: They've got the measure of the seamers. They'll soon begin chasing points.

Glump: Points? What points?

Doornail: Bobby Abel was a good point, too.

Puter (patronisingly to Glump): Surely you know? They've introduced a new system of points.

Nowall: Splendid innovation. A side gets two points if it compiles so many runs in a given number of overs or something.

Puter: Over and above a certain total.

Nowall: Yes, or gets so many wickets before the batting side has notched a certain number of runs before losing the number of wickets in question.

Puter: Or more.

Nowall: Naturally. So many more for more. And still fifteen points for an outright win. I don't know why they haven't altered that yet.

Glump: Oh, good lord. How the devil does a captain keep a reckoning?

Nowall: I'm not quite sure; but he does. Because it enables him to declare when he's trailing on the first innings. Prevents the opponents snatching a brace of points.

Glump: Why?

Puter: What? Well – anyhow, it's done the game a world of good. And it's very popular. Both with players and public.

Glump: Oh. It sounds a lot of damn nonsense to me.

(*pause*)

Glump: I've never seen a slower bat than this chap. Have you?

Doornail: Well, not since W.G. Quaife.

Nowall: Give him a chance, sir. The spinners have now taken up the attack . . . (*to Puter*): Think it's taking spin?

Puter: Slowly if at all. But I've seen one or two drift.

Nowall: He's doing a bit both ways from this end.

Puter: Yes and not too easy to read.

Doornail: Read? Ah, now, W.W. Read. He was a good slogger.

Glump: I wish to hell this feller was.

Puter: Ah, but he's essentially a front foot player.

Glump: He's got two feet, hasn't he? Why can't he jump out and hit it over their heads?

Nowall: Daren't risk that. He might be a fraction late and spoon a gaper to deep mid-off.

Doornail: Spooner. Now there was a stylist if you like.

Glump: Anyhow, he's out now. Clean lbw.

Puter: No, no. Front pad. And he was well forward on the prod.

Nowall: And probably missing the leg stump.

Puter: Besides, he looked to me to have got a tickle.

Glump: Well, all I can say is they ought to alter the lbw rule.

Nowall: They talk of doing that, to counteract the prod.

Puter: Yes. I agree the poor old lbw law is obsolete.

Nowall: Absolutely. It's been the same for about two seasons.

Glump: (*rising with difficulty*): Well, I think I shall feel more at home in the long bar. Why doesn't this bowler have another chap at short fine leg?

Puter: He's only allowed two behind the umpire. Five fielders on the onside altogether.

Doornail: Fielder once took all ten wickets for the Players.

Norwall (to Puter): Does that still hold good?

Puter: Yes, doesn't it?

Nowall: I wasn't sure. They keep changing the regulations so . . .

Puter: Steady. It's all for the good of the game.

Glump: What is? Let alone changing the regulations – no points for this, points for that instead – nobody knows how many points or what for. This and that and the other. What's it all *for*?

Puter: That's an easy one. It's to induce more people to spend a good deal more money to come and spend the day watching county cricket. That is, of course, when it's not raining.

Glump: And *is* it indoocing 'em?

Puter: Well, I suppose it's what you might call a long-term policy.

Nowall: Oh, make no mistake, it's all a grand thing for players and public alike. Makes cricket a more exhilarating and popular game all round.

Doornail: I'll tell you who was a good all-rounder – Moses.

(Winter Annual 1968–69)

DREAM ELEVENS

WASHERWOMEN
By Michael Meyer

The washerwomen of cricket – those, I mean, whose chief occupation in connection with the game is the compiling of lists – have been strangely silent of late. I think the last really ingenious team to be published was one whose members all wore moustaches. Only living cricketers were, of course, included; fifty years ago, it would have been almost equally difficult to pick a clean-shaven eleven, although the young Clem Hill would have been an immediate choice.

This picking of teams with an eye to non-geographical qualifications serves a double purpose; it familiarises one with the bizarrely named old players who lie shrouded in *Wisden* among the Births and Deaths; and it renovates familiar names, polishing and burnishing them so that new facets catch our eye. Mr Cardus's famous essay, *What's in a Name*, in which he selected teams with lovely and unlovely names, showed us the great in most unexpected postures. C.B. Fry appeared, as though in a *montage* picture, doling chips from a vat of batter with a wire ladle; and Wilfred Rhodes seemed presented against a background, not of rocky moorland, but of broken columns and quiet seas.

Virgin paper oblong
The MCC authorities have assisted us energetic washerwomen by removing the list of fixtures from the back of the Lord's scorecards, thereby presenting us with the irresistible temptation of a virgin paper oblong; and on August Monday the Australian cricketers provided the correct sober backcloth for a creative mood. The usual sources of perplexity – alphabetical elevens, county amateurs, etc. – were exhausted long before the patience of Squadron Leader Sismey, whose monodic accompani-

ment kept the mind on its narrow track, as a steady drumbeat drills a soldier into unresisting obedience. Soon the following meal appeared (in eating order); and I challenge anyone to put a better on to the field.

Grace: Place (Lancs); Pepper; Partridge (Northants); Beet, G.H. (wkt); Mead; Duff, R.A.; Bakewell; Peach; Parkin; Hazell.

Parkin is a cake of oatmeal and treacle. Hazell might seem an anti-climax at the end of such a splendid feast, but I requre a left-hander, and besides, he is a Somerset man. Fry, I think, just fails to qualify – it would mean dropping a course – and so does Cutmore, for the same reason. The Rev. Sir F.L. Currie, 2nd Bart (Cambridge U., born 1823) would add distinction, and he could be accompanied by Surgeon-Lieutenant D. Rice. I thought of trying to select a 2s. 6d. meal, headed by these two, and including Peel and Worthington, but cannot complete the eleven, unless I incorporate 'after-dinner comforts', in which case we have the following excellent side: E.L. Kidd; Cutmore; The Rev. Sir F.L. Currie; Surgeon-Lieut. D. Rice; Peel; Fagg; Thursting (Leics); Beveridge; J.C. Clay; Paine – and my eleventh man, a capital left-hand batsman, must remain unprinted for reasons of modesty. Fagg would be my wicket-keeper, unless that was the Rev. Currie's department.

A match I would like to see would be Tradesmen v Lords and Masters, between, e.g.: Tradesmen – Paynter; J.A. Workman; Barber; K. Miller; J.R. Mason; Shepherd, T.W.; Cooper, E.; Pothecary; Smith, E. J. (wkt); C.T.B. Turner; Ironmonger. Lords and Masters – J.B. King; D.J. Knight; Squires; Cook (nowadays); G.F. Earle; I.F. Bishop; Pope, G.H.; Dean, H.; Butler (see Cook); M.A. Noble; Judge.

Animals v Birds

Animals and Birds I found surprisingly difficult, and Animals, despite the inclusion of two obscure nineteenth-century Blues, remain incomplete, awaiting the assistance of some more knowledgeable reader. Birds – Lord Hawke; Dipper; Martin, S.H.; M.C. Bird; R.W.V. Robins; N.E. Partridge; Drake, E.J.; D.F. Cock; M. Falcon; Woodcock, A. (Leics); H. Sparrow. Animals – Bull (Worcs); Fox, J. (Warwicks and Worcs); M.D. Lyon; B.H. Lyon; Gibbons, H.H.; E.L. Kidd (again); H.J.H. Lamb; J.H.M. Hare; H. Pigg; Hart.

Mr Sparrow's main distinction was to live to the age of 95. He played for Warwickshire and Worcestershire. The Birds would also benefit by the experience of John Crow (1847–1939), Kent scorer from 1874–96. Mr Hare got his Oxford Blue in 1879, while Mr Pigg, hailing from Abingdon House School, Northampton, played for Cambridge two years earlier. There is a Woof, but no Wolf; and disappointingly, no representative of the various breeds of dogs.

I had just made a promising start on 'Weapons and Implements' with Gimblett, Gunn, A.W.H. Mallett and D.C.G. Raikes, when Sismey was hit on the hand by Pollard, and retired. For the rest of the day, *real cricket* occupied my attention; and my dream elevens continued their misty contests without an audience.

(Annual, 1945–46)

SPECTACLED CRICKETERS

Dear Sir,

When Surrey met Essex at the Oval, there were four players on the field all wearing glasses, *viz*.: – Kirby, McMahon and Pratt of Surrey and Gibb of Essex! I am wondering whether this is a record, or whether any of your readers can recall a parallel.

In this connection, some years ago, I compiled a team of spectacled cricketers of all time, which the late Mr. E.H.D. Sewell did me the honour of mentioning in his book *Overthrows*. It was as follows: – R.A. Young, W.G. Grace Jr, Rev. J.H. Parsons, M. Howell, H.S. Squires, J. N. Crawford, P.A. Gibb, E.H. Killick, T.B. Mitchell, H.R. Bromley, E.H. Davenport, W.E. Bowes.

Is it possible to select a spectacled XI from those now playing? I am not sufficiently familiar with the majority of players and can only think of Dovey (Kent), and Harrison (Hampshire) in addition to those mentioned above.

Yours etc.,
GEOFFREY MORTON
133 Nether Street,
London, N.12
(1953)

THE - EYS OF CRICKET

Sir,

I have been interested to note the number of present-day first-class cricketers whose names end in - EY, and I have compiled a list of such players from which quite a strong team could be picked. R.N. Abberley (Warwicks), W.E. Alley (Somerset), R.R. Bailey (Northants), T.E. Bailey (Essex), M.C. Cowdrey (Kent), K. Gilhouley (Notts), T.W. Graveney (Worcs), R.G.A. Headley (Worcs), R.G. Humphrey (Surrey, wkt), J.F. Harvey (Derbys), C.T. Radley (Middlesex), M.J. Smedley (Notts), F.E. Rumsey (Somerset), K.J. Wheatley (Hants), O.S. Wheatley (Glamorgan), D.S. Worsley (Lancashire), S.J. Storey (Surrey), G.N.S. Ridley (Oxford U. and Kent), and Peter Willey (Northants).

The only really 'untried' member of the party is the one and only wicket-keeper, R.G. Humphrey, understudy to Arnold Long, the regular Surrey stumper.

S. CANYNGE CAPLE
Tredrea Meadow,
Church Road,
Perran-Ar-Worthal,
Truro, Cornwall
(1966)

FRAGMENTS
By R.C. Robertson-Glasgow

. . . How often do we see alternative teams – shoals of them – suggested as liable 'to give a good game' to the already chosen England, Players or Gentlemen XI, 'to set them furiously to think.' Now I propose the following sides as liable to give a game to no team in the world, but to plunge anyone – Gentleman or Player – into most furious thought. We will call the match Impossibles versus Improbables, inasmuch as it is impossible that any one of them should ever be chosen, and improbable that, once chosen, they would justify selection.

Impossibles – Krassin (captain), Israel Zangwill, Jack Jones, Freeman, Hardy, Willis, Baron Orczy, Saklatvala, Michael Arlen, Hindenburg, Capablanca. 12th man, De Valera.

Improbables – Mussolini (captain), President Coolidge, Debenham, Freebody, Boguslavsky, Bernard Shaw, the Emir Feisul, Augustus John, M. Painlevé, Keating and D. Lloyd George. 12th man, Epstein.

And thus would we summarise their respective chances:' We think that either of these sides would seriously tax an England XI. Krassin's leadership has long been recognised (except by the present Government) as inspiring and original, though at times unorthodox. As a set-off to Tate's devastating "nip" from the wicket, we would have Baron Orczy's left-hand expresses, Hindenburg's insidious slows and the Emir Feisul's length deliveries; whilst Debenham's curious corkscrew run from behind the umpire might upset the calculations of the most experienced exponent of the willow, and it is well known that Augustus John always keeps an extra special ball in reserve up his beard. Israel Zangwill will hit the ball to Jericho and back, Capablanca is conversant with every move in the game, Freebody always has the measure of his man, Jack Jones knows the Obstruction Rule from A to Z and may be relied upon to appeal loudly on all occasions. Lloyd George at will can give the batsman out by a successful mimicry of the umpire's voice, Saklatvala can stay at home till Domesday, Michael Arlen plays a bold, if risky, game, while President Coolidge's stationary dignity at cover-point will be an object of admiration to all. Strudwick, too, will have to look to his laurels when Mussolini is behind the stumps; for there are more unlikely things than that the Italian Aunt Sally will pouch several snicks, or concede a caught-and-bowled off his stomach. Anyhow, we should like to see either, or the pick, of these two sides play an England XI.' We should *very* much like to see it.

(Annual, 1925–26)

A TEAM OF CRICKETING ECCENTRICS
By M.H. Stevenson

I know a man who's so keen on cricket that he spends a fair number of his waking hours selecting teams – 'The Best Ever XI of Parsons', 'Teams of Players with Common Initial Letters', 'World XI's', 'An XI of Left-Handers', 'A Team of Yorkshire Exiles', and the award-winning 'Team of Fatties!' Thus it was largely a matter of self-defence that prompted me to select my own XI of 'Cricketing Characters', encountered during a fairly lengthy and vastly enjoyable series of cricket wanderings.

It is a tribute to the game we know and love so well ('hearts and flowers' music off-stage) that so many candidates present themselves for selection. Accordingly, as always, the final choice presented considerable problems. I have not allowed mere lack of survival to rule anyone out and, if selected, one can presume that any lover of cricket will be only too delighted to return as a shade, to do battle for this most entertaining of sides.

Now for a Good "Opening"!

Dewar's
"White Label"
Scotch that stands any Test

Incidentally I imagine that the immense number of oddities, eccentrics and plain weirdies that adorn, and have adorned, the game of cricket, as against other sports, is easily accounted for in terms of sheer time, not only profitably used for rehearsal of ploys, pranks and pixillations but also in that the generally more leisurely unfolding of the contest over a considerable period creates circumstances out of which humorous development is inevitable. Put rather differently, it is hard to imagine 'X' formulating witticisms while running onto a through pass at Wembley or 'Y' concentrating on anything other than the job in hand as he attempts to side-step through at Twickenham; but standing next to Arthur Mitchell, 'Cec' Pepper or F.S.T. in slips or leg-trap – that's quite another matter!

My number one in the batting order is unquestionably Willie Andrews, alas no longer with us. What a legend he became in Irish cricket and above all at Lord's! There he would, until recently, rarely miss his practice stint, watching behind the wicket for safety, with a critical glare if any enthusiastic young bowler forgot the relative vulnerability of his 70 years!

Willie must have been one of the keenest cricketers who ever lived. In his youth, the story has it, he was playing in a Belfast League game and was at the non-striking end, while a fearsome fast bowler operated mercilessly and devastingly. At last a colleague of Willie was struck a truly terrible blow on the head and began to stagger around more or less on a length with a good deal of blood issuing from between agonised fingers which clutched the injury. All and sundry clustered around to minister to him or, more morbidly, to assess the extent of the damage. Not so Willie, who remained erect and impassive at the bowler's end, calling anxiously in his rather high-pitched Ulster voice, 'Don't fall on your wicket, don't fall on your wicket!' The batsman did not play again that season.

I played with Willie, who was in his mid-seventies at the time, for MCC v Giggleswick. He insisted on fielding on the boundary so that he could hear the current Test match on a transistor there. The school's wickets fell and a thin, anxious youth was attempting to dig the old Alma Mater out of trouble, when the sky darkened, a hush fell on the ground and Willie, making around one and a half to two knots, arrived breathless at the wicket. 'Australia 187 for 6,' he said. 'I thought you'd like to know.' He departed and the pale youth was instantly bowled, not having previously experienced anything quite like this in a school match; we were soon in the pub!

His opening partner was a colleague in the press-box at Aigburth last summer on the occasion of Lancashire's match with Sussex. Michael Buss, fair-haired and slow-medium, came on to purvey his little left-arm floaters and seamers, whereupon my fellow reporter leant across to me nervously and enquired, 'Is it David Snow?'

Bramall Lane barrackers

At number three I would like to select a job-lot of vintage Bramall Lane barrackers, represented by the one about whom Charlie Lee tells a fine story. As a Yorkshire exile he was very few indeed not out, following around 90 minutes' batting one Saturday evening at Sheffield, and just before close of play, a voice from the crowd asked, 'Arta coomin' Moonda, Charlie?' Charlie waved an affirmative bat and the voice replied, 'Ah'm bloody not!'

To fill the crucial number four postion, somebody of sobriety and typical British phlegm is needed, so of course we must have John Warr. (He always fancied himself as a batsman!) So much has been spoken and written about him that I will confine my remarks to a belated apprecia-tion of the four seasons' coaching in *Basic Funneys* plus an introduction to *The Poor Man's Practical Joker's Instant Success Kit for Aspiring Humorists*, which I underwent during our time together in the Cambridge side. Incidentally, I've often wondered if it could have been Charlie Lee's barracker who enquired sympathetically of John, who was fielding on the boundary at Bramall Lane, following a disastrously unsuccessful match for Middlesex against Yorkshire, 'Have yer coom oop 'ere to 'ave yer pen-knife sharpened?'

Nude with cap and pipe

At five I've selected Billy Featherby, not entirely because of his unusual habit of removing every stitch of clothing in the dressing-room before a match, putting on his cricket cap, then lighting his pipe, but also to provide the opportunity of quoting from a letter which Billy received just before his death, from Emmott Robinson. 'Grunds is 'ard. Us is tired and umpires won't give us out.' Umpires have finally given Emmott out, but after a magnificent innings. I imagine that the presence of a poetic talent

A TEAM OF DEMONS.

of this calibre in one of the dourest of Yorkshire's legendary cricketing characters will come as something of a surprise to many folk.

Dick Greenwood is my number six. Many people will know him as one of the country's leading Rugby brains but his cricketing talents may not be so widely known. His extreme enthusiasm is easily illustrated. Last season he bowled me out (not in any way a noteworthy event) during a Wagnerian thunderstorm and with a background of Californian Red-woods during an evening match at Stonyhurst. While still totally airborne he was heard to howl with primeval triumph, 'What a prune, what a prune!'

Some time ago, while batting with Nick Drake-Lee, the England prop forward, he went for a short run and dived from around ten yards, knocking over stumps and umpire in the process. When Dick recovered the power of speech he said to the umpire, as no appeal for a run-out had been made, 'That must have been close. Was I out?' 'Yes,' said the umpire, no doubt still incensed at the unprovoked assault – and he had to go!

At seven we have the Irish umpire I once met, who, when the batsman snicked the ball firmly on to his front leg 18 inches outside his leg stump, was the only person on the field to appeal – and sportsman enough to turn it down!

Which brings me to Dick Howarth of Worcestershire, England and the Palladium. Hearing Dick on the subject of a certain colleague in the county side is one of my abiding cricketing memories, as is his lugu-briously tuneless singing of 'Dewes and Sheppard can't play spin' to the tune of 'Nymphs and shepherds come away', having done considerable execution on the Cambridge batting.

Choc-Ice man from Fenner's

At number nine, as any keen follower of the game knows, it is vital to have a man who possesses iron nerve, enterprise and vitality coupled with that admirable team spirit which makes a person ready to serve in a subordinate role. With these qualities in mind I have selected the Choc-Ice man from Fenner's who so often earned a round of admiring applause from the players for the speed and accuracy of his pick-up and throw, after he had downed his tray of ices, his virtuosity being especially appreciated on the occasion of the West Indies' scoring about 700 runs against the University in 1952, aided by a scratchy 300-odd from Everton Weekes.

At ten we have Mr R.J.O. Meyer, the present Headmaster of Millfield and late of Somerset CCC. He is selected not because he gave me a charming but totally uncompromising dressing-down for rubbing my

48

shoulder ostentatiously, when given caught behind on 48 following my first innings at Lord's, the ball having hit my shirt, but because he played the most remarkable innings that it has been my privilege to see. When Jack came to the wicket, the Somerset Stragglers were in real trouble against my own Old Boys' team, the Rydal Dolphins. When their number eleven appeared their score was at about 90 for 9 and there the day ended.

Shortly before lunch on the second day, if my memory serves me correctly, Jack Meyer was about 150 not out, when his loyal colleague was dismissed for nine. He had employed a variety of strokes that would have drawn admiring gasps from Jonah Barrington, Arnold Palmer and Virginia Wade, and had he applied the same approach during his distinguished career in education that he brought to his batting on this occasion, Millfield would have degenerated into a cross between Grey-friars and Dotheboys Hall!

At number eleven I have chosen a Mr P.B.H. May, largely for the pleasure of seeing him bat in this position but also to commemorate the fact that, until he became captain of England and subjected to the hard glare of the spotlight of publicity, I had never heard anyone say a single harsh word about him; and then, the only criticism that I heard was that some found him remote. Hmph! If Peter May is guilty of remoteness, it's a pity that a few more don't try it!

Come to think of it, if this team ever takes the field, our main worry will be the certainty of jealous complaints from Equity!

(Spring Annual, 1970)

'I suppose this means a victory parade through the streets of London and a service of thanksgiving in St. Paul's.'

(1968)

49

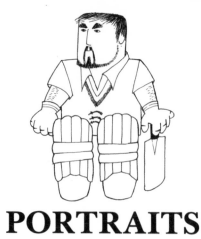

PORTRAITS

IT WAS AS IF THE SUN HAD BROKEN THROUGH
By A.P. Singleton

The cricket season of 1934, my first at Oxford, opened with bitterly cold weather and grey skies. It was also apparent to those of us who had any aspirations to get into the University team, that the cricket was going to be conducted on austere lines. The various authorities, resident and imported, who controlled the conduct of affairs on the field seemed to have a fixation for physical fitness, the cleaner, better life, early to bed and early to rise, and a general disregard for the more light-hearted and humorous side of cricket. I think that the majority of us felt that the whole thing was being conducted far too much like a Test match campaign.

Then, one day, the whole atmosphere changed. This was partly due to the retirement of our honorary coaches to other duties, but mostly to the arrival on the scene of one of the most remarkable characters I ever met. I was at the nets at the time, and so saw him at once, for the nets are beside the approach path to the pavilion. He approached with swinging yet springy gait, and looked like a character, even from a distance.

He was dressed, reading from south to north, in what looked like rather an elderly pair of dancing shoes, blue socks, one with a large potato in the heel, a pair of wide grey flannels, worn at half mast, a sports coat held open by his left hand which was in his trousers pocket, the arm also supporting *The Morning Post*, a far from new shirt, and a tie which had blown back over his shoulder. Surmounting all this was a bronzed face, rather like that of a Red Indian, containing the most humorous and sparkling pair of grey eyes I have seen. I was amazed, and awed, to find that this was the famous Somerset bowler and cricket writer, R.C. Robertson-Glasgow, and this was the beginning of a close friendship which lasted for many years.

Gales of laughter

From the moment he arrived in the Parks, it was as if the sun had at last broken through. There were gales of laughter, led by his own stentorian bellow, amusing stories, and incidents by the dozen. Even the most serious-minded could not help joining in and laughing. He joined with us in the nets, and reported our cricket on the field with a kindly humour totally lacking in today's cricket writings, and, best of all, he treated us, not much more than schoolboys, as equals.

This became an annual event, his arrival at the Parks, and we all looked forward to it. Officially he was there to report on the trials and the early matches, and he carried in a side pocket of his sports coat one of those 6d. red memo books from Woolworths. This he referred to as 'The washing book', and this he would put on the mantelpiece in the pavilion, with a stub of pencil, with the remark, 'I've put the washing book up there. If anything happens, shove it in. I'm off to the nets.' And away he would go, while we entered the relevant details of the match in progress. His report the following morning was always most accurate, and full of humour.

After the day's play we would repair to Vincent's club more often than not for a pint or two of beer, and this was when he was at his best, and he would regale us with stories and memories, and occasionally his poetry, which was brilliant but, unfortunately, unprintable. But he was never a bore and I never knew anyone who did not welcome him except, possibly, one local, rather stuffy headmaster who thought that he should not be allowed in the club during the term as he was bad for the undergraduates; this opinion, I need hardly say, was unsupported. The talk was mainly concerned with cricket and golf, for Crusoe, as we all knew him, was a great theorist, especially about bowling.

I remember one February when he came up to report a golf match and duly appeared in the club on the Saturday evening – we agreed to lunch on the Sunday in the 'George'. This was a good lunch, washed down by several pints of bitter, attended by half a dozen or so of us in the warm and friendly atmosphere of the 'George', while the snow drifted down outside. There was a great deal of noise and laughter, and the conversation inevitably turned to cricket and swing bowling. Crusoe was laying down the law about field placing, and we did not all agree. So he decided that the only solution was a practical demonstration, and with that he ordered half a dozen rolls and we all went down into the street outside, which had lamp-posts at intervals in the middle of the street.

Crusoe placed his field and himself opened the bowling with a roll from the station end, with a lamp post as the wicket, and Mitchell-Innes taking strike using an umbrella as a bat. The game progressed for a while, possibly a little informally but with a great deal of noise and

Said a batsman called Oliver Lees,

" This bowler aims straight at my knees."

But Schweppes Tonic so lashed

Him to zeal that he smashed

All the scorer's front teeth out with ease.

Schweppes
TONIC WATER
- does you Good

(1935)

laughter, with the snow still falling, and then a policeman appeared on the scene and asked what was going on. Glasgow at once approached him and, in his charming and forthright way, pointed out that we were doing harm to no-one, and that there was very little traffic anyway, and that the policeman could do us a great service by acting as umpire, for which job he was admirably suited. To our surprise, the policeman laughed and took up this position and joined in the general fun. Such was Crusoe's personality.

Wonderful evening

He had a disarming lack of formality which saw him through almost any scrape. I remember one wonderful evening. He asked me to dine as his guest at the Savage Club, and assured me that it would be perfectly all right to leave the car in Waterloo Place, just round the corner. This was a great occasion in my life; the guests including Sir Jack Hobbs, Sir Malcolm Campbell, and many other of my heroes. Also were present the Western Brothers, Starr Wood, Billy Bennett and others from the stage, all of whom did turns. I also remember Vivian Jenkins and Arthur Rees of the Welsh Rugby team, and men of colossal muscle and build, teaching Andy Sandham the elementary principles of rugger in a marble hall with pillars in it. Sandham was sober and nippy enough to keep out of harm's way, but how the other two survived serious injury, or even death, I never understood.

This was at about 2 am and we then went out to the car. A lone policeman was sitting on the running board, waiting for us. On arrival we asked him if there was anything wrong, and he pointed out that this was a two-hour park, and drew out his notebook. Crusoe asked him how it would be if we sloshed him and then drove away. The policeman replied that it would not be advisable 'as I happen to be the heavyweight champion of the Metropolitan Police!' This made everyone laugh so much that the policeman laughed too, and forgot all about the summons.

He also lacked formality in his dress; in fact, looking back on it, I cannot remember seeing him really well dressed, even in formal evening attire; somehow he always looked as if he had just arrived from a previous party, and a pretty rough one at that. Mrs Chapman once told me of a weekend visit to their house by Crusoe. He came down for a golf weekend, and Percy met him at the station. His sole luggage was a bag of museum type golf clubs and a large cabin trunk. This was in midwinter. With difficulty the trunk was manhandled on to the luggage carrier at the back of the car and later into the house. They then settled down to tea and hot buttered toast. During this, the maid knocked on the door and asked if she could speak to Madam. Mrs Chapman went out and asked the trouble, to which the maid replied that she was in a bit of a quandary as to what to do about Mr Glasgow's luggage, as the sole contents of the cabin trunk was a dirty pair of cricket boots.

Such, then, are some of my memories of Crusoe. He was very clever, but never heavy. It was impossible for people to be serious or morbid in his presence, and there was almost always a lot of noise where he was, with his own tremendous laugh dominating the scene. He was welcome wherever he went. I never met anyone who disliked him, and I do not remember him saying anything unpleasant about anyone. Above all, he was young at heart, and he had the ability to get on with young people and to make them think that they counted. As a cricket writer, the last thing he would have considered was sensationalism; he became famous in this sphere purely by the charm and humour of his writing.

(1965)

A KING WITHOUT A CROWN . . .
By R.C. Robertson-Glasgow

Biographies and essays have been written about celebrities, fools, crooks, bores, and exhibitionists; but, so far as I know, no-one has written a short book (he'd never stand for a *long* one) on Arthur A. Mailey, one of the great personalities of the lasty fifty or sixty years.

That he played cricket, as a leg-break-cum-googly bowler for New South Wales and Australia, is merely incidental. As a Test match bowler, he ranks among the great. But, as a man, he already stands, for those who have had the wonderful luck to know him, among the immortals.

I first met Arthur Mailey in May of 1921, on the Christ Church cricket ground at Oxford. I was to bat, more or less, at No. 11. Behind the stumps that day was the brilliant, neat, and courteous wicket-keeper, Bert Oldfield. The bowler that mattered was Mailey.

He smiled as I came in, a wide and sympathetic smile. He has always, I fancy, regarded batting as a necessary but inferior part of cricket. He had reason, this time, I knew, and he guessed that I knew nothing at all about the art of playing leg-spin bowling of quality. No discernment.

So, he smiled; and bowled three high and harmless non-spinners just outside the off stump. I swished at them, and three times connected. Mailey had deliberately presented me with twelve runs.

Then he had me stumped by a wide margin of space and time. '*Enjoyed yourself?*' he said, as we walked in. That was Arthur Mailey; the giver of good things; especially to the young and ignorant.

The millionaire bowler

In the preceding Australian season he had taken 36 wickets during a Test series against England, in spite of missing the second of the five matches, at Melbourne. As to technique, he used his broad strong fingers to impart spin even on the truest surface; and he was ever a lover of experimental flight. He has been called 'the millionaire bowler', because he was willing to 'buy' a wicket at a price.

Remember, too, that in those Australian teams of 1920 and 1921 there were runs to spare in the bank. Not till 1926, eight years after the end of the First Great War, did England's cricket catch up with Australia's. It is also worth remembering that in quite a number of Tests J.M. Gregory and E.A. McDonald, that great pair of fast bowlers, made Mailey's job hardly necessary.

This is not meant to be an exhaustive description of Mailey the cricketer. But it should be recorded that he took 9 for 121 in 47 overs in the Fourth Test against our 1920–21 team at Melbourne, including the wickets of Jack Hobbs, Wilfred Rhodes, and Frank Woolley; that in 1921 he took all 10 Gloucestershire wickets in their second innings at Cheltenham, including that of a boy called Walter Hammond, who was greatly to trouble Australian bowlers and batsmen in after years. And that in December 1924, at Sydney, he shared with J.M. Taylor (108) in a last-wicket Test stand of 127. Mailey's own score at No. 11 was 46 not out. They say he still laughs disbelievingly when the feat is mentioned.

But, with all respect to Australia, which has bred so many great, and some rather grim, games-players, she has produced only one Arthur Mailey.

He is so different from the typical Aussie player of games or runner of races. In Mailey, humour ranks higher than success, kindness above personal triumph. Not in money, but verily in character he is the richest man that his country has produced. There is something still of Huckleberry Finn about him, something of the boy who interrupts adventure to help or to laugh.

He is free from worry, because, not having made precise arrangements, he cannot be disappointed by any lack of their success. I remember that he never used to look up the starting-time of a train. He went to the station and waited for the next one in. As the years passed, he became even more of a will-o'-the-wisp; not to be pinned down; difficult to track.

Considerably gifted as an artist, he has been a professional cartoonist as well as a Test cricket reporter. Typically, in his cartoons, his own face has often been the funniest feature. But his greatest delight, I think, has been to paint in watercolours the English countryside in summer; the fruit-country, the Evenlode, and the severer beauties of the North.

Poet at large

For such expeditions he used a car with the necessary appurtenances for painting and sitting and sleeping. And he would leave behind no address for forwarding correspondence. The poet was at large.

And poet he is, though I doubt if he has ever written a sonnet or even a couplet. When he was a young man, he once took the wicket of his hero, the only Victor Trumper. So far from regarding this as a triumph, he said '*I felt as if I'd shot a dove.*'

Many are the stories, true or fanciful, about Arthur Mailey. The one that I like best is of moderately recent date, and refers to his starting a meat business in the purlieus of Sydney with a large placard above his shop on which he had written his name, then – '*used to bowl tripe; used to write tripe; now he sells tripe.*'

I fear we may not see Arthur Mailey over here in the 1964 summer. He is 75 years old, and has retired from the work of commentary and drawing. But, wherever he is, he will, I know, be encouraging the young and hopeful, and helping the old and despairing. Anyhow, for me Arthur Mailey is the greatest man I've ever met in cricket. A king without a crown.

(1963)

"HAVE YOU SEEN THESE
Crookes Halibut Oil advertisements ?"

(1951)

THE OTHER DOCTOR
By A.A. Thomson

Who was cricket's most illustrious doctor? The question is too easy, and there are no prizes for the answer. The next most renowned GP was W.G.'s brother, Edward Mills Grace, the robust and rumbustious E.M., a truly prodigious character. But setting aside the six doctors (father and five sons) of the Grace family, I am thinking of another sporting practitioner.

His first name, like that of so many good men, was Arthur and, though he had indulged in pastimes as exuberantly varied as boxing, football (both codes), golf, billiards, ski-ing, flying in its early stages, and whaling, cricket was his dearest love. Apart from the playful buckling of a couple of ribs at rugger, all his best wounds were inflicted by a cricket ball. Love is a most irrational emotion and Arthur, an Irishman born in Scotland, behaved all through like a typical Englishman, in preferring the game that hit him hardest. He played football till well on the wrong side of 40 and cricket till on the wrong side of 50. Then a fast bowler battered him twice on the same knee and that ended his innings.

He learned his cricket the hard way and its first impact upon him (like its last) was a fearful blow on the knee-cap. This occurred at his prep school and, as he passed out, overwhelmed with the pain of it, little Arthur smiled happily. The blow had been struck by a popular professional cricketer, batting against the school. What brought the victim complete rapture was the composite fact that he had been knocked out by the mighty Tom Emmett and that Tom and his captain were reverently carrying him off to the school sanatorium.

His keenness on cricket at school was a byword; at medical school he could not give much time to the summer game, though he played for his university at rugger, gaining a reputation as a fast, heavy forward. He did not flash with meteor flight into the cricket sky, like W.G. or E.M., but worked his passage towards first-class status along the game's humbler, if more entertaining, byways.

Against the Gentlemen of Warwickshire, for instance, he once took three wickets in three balls and was presented with a dainty little silver hat, despite his third victim's protest that he had expected the ball to come from the bowler's left hand and, when it came from his right, it completely put him off his stroke. On another occasion, he clean bowled an artistically minded batsman, who appealed, not to the umpire, but to high heaven: 'How can one bat against a fellow with a crude pink shirt-sleeve against a positively agonizing olive-green background?'

Dutchmen not pull-men

In a low-level international match at The Hague in the Nineties he played a hero's part for a wandering English XI against a strong Dutch side, which contained a redoubtable bowler. This was C.J. Posthuma, who may or may not have been the Dutch W.G., but certainly enjoyed a reputation as the local equivalent of the Old Man. He was himself an ebullient character and the fact that he called his three dogs W.G., C.B., (after Fry) and Archie (after A.C. MacLaren) was not the only evidence of his interest in cricket. He also came over regularly and played for W.G.'s London County side. As a bowler he was slow, left-handed, with a colossal break that could pitch off the matting, and then with a sudden lateral leap, shatter your wicket. Against this dangerous character Arthur evolved an ingenious strategy: this consisted of exploiting his knowledge that the Dutchmen had been trained by an honest English coach to play everything 'straight' and never descend to the agricultural inelegance of pulling. He therefore packed his off-side and had half the opposing side caught at cover. His delighted comrades carried him shoulder-high into the pavilion and then, inconsequently, dropped all 16 stone of him.

He played with J.M. Barrie's fantastic XI, the Allah-Akbarries, eccentric souls who had a note printed on their visiting cards:
Practice ground: Editorial Office, the National Observer.

In one match he nearly made history. The Allah-Akbarries had made 72 and had taken nine enemy wickets for exactly the same total. At this point Arthur started to bowl. There were indignant cries from the pavilion and the entire batting side emerged, arguing fiercely. Arthur you see, was the only real bowler on the side and at this critical juncture, in sheer excitement, he was beginning a new over, having just taken his ninth wicket with his last ball at the other end. Arthur always claimed to be the first bowler to attempt this (though by accident) and was deeply hurt when a quarter of a century later Warwick Armstrong stole his thunder by doing the same thing in a Test match. Besides, Arthur was not allowed to bowl his second over, anyway. With his opponents swarming round him, rule-books in hand, Arthur dropped the ball. To prevent a riot, another bowler was put on and the enemy won forthwith by a wide and four overthrows.

It was not until the first decade of this century that Arthur achieved his great ambition of playing first-class cricket for the best part of a season, making good scores against the leading counties, including Kent and Derbyshire, and finishing with the creditable batting average of 32. He took a modest pride in his ability to hold his place in a good MCC side as an amateur bowler, because bowling at that time was almost invariably a professional's job.

Arthur liked to tell, for he had a certain talent as a story-teller, of the three most disconcerting deliveries he received during his first-class career. The first was from W.G. Arthur had compiled a stylish 30-odd, culminating in a handsome on-drive for four, and stepped briskly out to take another off the next ball. It looked exactly the same, but the Old Man had cunningly flighted it, so that it rose a little higher and dropped a little shorter and Arthur was politely but remorselessly stumped by another Arthur – Arthur Augustus Lilley. That was a favourite ball of W.G.'s, childlike, blank and deceitful as sin itself.

A ball that bothered Arthur even more than W.G.'s Chinese donkey-drop came to him in the form of a dive-bombing attack from A. P. Lucas, the eminent Cambridge, Essex and England cricketer, who should have known better. Apparently he tossed up a 30-foot lob, which would have been more at home at Wimbledon than at Lord's. As the ball came slowly but menacingly, Arthur pondered deeply on the problem of defending his citadel against this dastardly attack. Should he boldly attempt to drive if? Should he play it more soberly with the upturned face of the bat? The ball seemed an eternity in descending. At what seemed the last moment he changed his mind and unleashed a powerful slash with the object of cutting the horrid thing past point. There was a crash of falling timber; two stumps and the blade of his bat flew in different directions. And as Arthur contemplated the wreckage, the ball descended on the remaining stump and knocked it sideways. Never, he reflected, had a batsman been dismissed so comprehensively.

Batsman on fire
The third most interesting delivery in his collection came from that tearaway fast bowler, that South-country Brearley, W. M. Bradley of Kent. The ball rose violently and hit the batsman on the thigh. The pain was sharp, but natural. Suddenly it became sharper and then wholly unbearable.

'My word, sir,' murmured the wicket-keeper respectfully, 'you're on fire.'

Arthur clapped his hand to the spot. The ball had hit a small tin box of matches in his trousers pocket and ignited them. Whirling like a Dervish, he snatched them out, hurled them away from the crease, and following with an agile spring, proceeded to dance on them. W.G. lumbered in from point. 'Ho,' he rumbled, 'couldn't get you out. Had to set you on fire.'

Even fiery Freddie Trueman never did that.

Arthur played cricket till long after this perilous escape, indeed as long as his knee would let him. Years afterwards he wrote: 'I have had as long an innings as one could reasonably expect and carry many pleasant friendships and recollections away with me . . .'

He was a fine type of cricketing doctor. He had other accomplishments, too, possessing, as I have said, some talent for story-telling.

His full name was Arthur Conan Doyle.

(1957)

The Gillette Cup Cricket Quiz 2

Which fast bowler swears by Foamy?

For over 200 years the laws of cricket have attempted to maintain an equilibrium between bat and ball and, for the same time, batsmen and bowlers have tried to upset it.

Bowlers, in particular, have included threats, glares and unshaven chins in their psychological armoury. Recently we heard of a paceman who foamed at the mouth when running up to bowl and was said to be buying cans of Foamy shaving cream by the gross.

"Foamy" he said when we asked him about it "...Rich creamy lather in an aerosol...Regular or Lemon-Lime from Gillette?" We nodded. "I swear by it!" he said. And he obviously did!

**Gillette Foamy
(Regular and Lemon-Lime)
chins swear by it**

(1976)

TALES MY TRUEMAN TOLD ME
By A.A. Thomson

A few people are characters. A few more are personalities. A few more still are somebody. It is no disgrace not to be any of these. The difficulty comes when . . . Well, one quiet day I was going past the back door of Lord's pavilion, doing no harm to a soul, when a small boy approached me diffidently, autograph album in hand.

'Excuse me,' he said, 'but are you . . . *anybody?*'

A sad moment. I thought for a moment of pretending I had played for England in 1909 – in that year practically anybody did. Happily I espied a member of the Middlesex Second XI approaching and, of course, when I introduced them, they were both happy. But it was a near-run thing.

While it is humiliating not to be *anybody*, it is nice to be a somebody, gratifying to be a personality (especially if you make well-paid television appearances), but it is a rare thing to be a character. We are constantly told that in cricket, as everywhere else, there are no characters nowadays. This is untrue. Of course there are characters in the game; not many, but then there never were so many as all that. Personalities there are in plenty, publicity being part of the machinery of modern life. Characters are different. Characters are not artificially inflated. They are real; they are human, humorous, earthy, and seldom willing martyrs to discipline. That they are more frequently found in the North is a matter of history, though it would be absurd to deny charactership to cricketers like, say, Patsy Hendren and Tony Lock. But the North country character comes of a long line of juicy eccentrics from Tom Emmett and 'Happy' Jack Ulyett to Emmott Robinson and Arthur Wood. And as heir to all these ages I nominate Frederick Sewards Trueman, one of the few figures today who can raise a roar of welcome wherever he goes.

29 wickets against India

Some players pass modestly on to the international scene. Sir Leonard Hutton got 0 and 1 in his first Test. But Trueman made his entry like the demon king in the pantomime. What he did to the Indian visitors in 1952 was not dismissal; it was destruction. In the series he captured 29 wickets, a record for a bowler's first rubber, and this bag included an eight for 31. There have been greater feats, if you think of Hedley Verity and, of course, Jim Laker, but seldom have a Test side been so demoralised. They were not so much bowled out as blasted out. Of the Leeds match *Wisden's* showed a scoreboard picture, 0–4–0, headed 'THE WORST START IN TEST CRICKET'. After the Manchester game (Trueman, eight for 31) he received high praise, except for a characteristic protest

61

from the chairman of the Old Trafford ground committee: 'Look, Freddie, you've got lots of pitches in Yorkshire, but if you keep on treading so heavily, Lancashire won't even have one!'

On this habit of heavy pounding hangs an apocryphal tale. On a wet spongy surface Trueman's footsteps were making only too deep an impression. 'Look, Freddie,' said the umpire, 'you're cutting up the turf something cruel. Why not try the other side for a change?'

Good-temperedly Freddie bowled a couple of overs round the wicket, but the umpire shook his head.

'That's just as bad, lad. You'd better go back to where you started.'

'All right,' said Freddie, 'but what have I to do to bowl here? Pass a driving test?'

What fast bowlers are for

A miner and the son of a miner, Trueman brought forthrightness and massive physical strength to the task of fast bowling. Though capable of subtlety and variation, he appears to take his richest pleasure in knocking your stumps flat, which, after all, is what fast bowlers are for. Trueman is a fast bowler with every muscle of his body, every glint of his bright eye, every lock of his thick black mane.

He is proud of his speed. Driving home from Headingley one evening, he was overtaken by a traffic policeman.

'Mr F.S. Trueman,' the officer read respectfully from the proffered driving licence. 'Are you by any chance the Yorkshire and England bowler?'

'That's right.'

'Then I'm afraid, sir, you were driving a lot faster than you bowl.'

'That I wasn't,' retorted Freddie. 'If I had been, you'd never have copped me.'

He appears self-confident to the point of cockiness (and, goodness, why not?) but I have heard him modestly ask, and accept, advice on technical matters from a famous fast bowler of earlier days. And he has been wise enough to benefit greatly by the answers.

From 1951, when he took five for 19 against the visiting South Africans and twice captured eight against Notts right up to last summer, when his five for 58 and six for 30 against the Australians at Leeds were among the few jewels in England's battered crown, he has bowled with heart, soul and stamina. In all he has taken 1,465 wickets, 1,098 of them for Yorkshire and 194 for England, and he has worked like a Trojan for every one. In the West Indies in 1959–60, just as in England in 1961, he was the architect of England's solitary victory. On reflection, architect is the wrong word. 'Foreman of the demolition squad' would be happier.

He and Brian Statham have been the great fast bowling pair of their era, well worthy to be named with earlier pairs of paladins: Lockwood and Richardson, Gregory and McDonald, Larwood and Voce, and Miller and Lindwall. To their partnership Statham has brought the steel and Trueman the fire; or, alternatively, if Statham claims the fire, Trueman undoubtedly supplies the brimstone.

Attack with Slazenger!

1960

Like any hero of old, Trueman figures in countless legends. Some are just stories which attach themselves to any flyaway fast bowler and were probably told about Brown of Brighton and Alfred Mynn. Some are apocryphal, but in a nice way. Quite a number are true. A larger number ought to be true. I have never myself invented one unless I have genuinely felt it *ought* to be true. In any event, legends do not accumulate by the dozen round a nonentity. His mode of expression is forceful. Hazlitt once said that to watch Kean act was to read Shakespeare by flashes of lightning. Conversation with Freddie can have a similar effect.

On the last Australian tour he was billeted in an unconscionably hot hotel room – I suspect Brisbane – where he was assailed by a vicious gang of mosquitoes. Rushing into the corridor, he sought the manager and demanded protection.

'It's the light that attracts them,' said the manager. 'Put your light out.'

Freddie retired and switched off his light; vainly, however, for the mosquitoes returned in force, with a squadron of glow-worms in close support. Out bounded the victim once more.

'What now?' demanded the manager. 'Didn't you put the light out?'

'Of course I did,' cried Freddie, 'but now they're looking for me with miners' lamps!'

His benefit match

In the Yorkshire County Cricket Club's current annual the following somewhat austere paragraph appears: 'F.S. Trueman has been granted a benefit during the forthcoming season, and has selected the Surrey match to be played at Sheffield on 30th June, 2nd and 3rd July as his benefit match. Members and friends are invited to help and make his reward worthy of his services for Yorkshire and England.'

This is a sober judgment on cricket's most techni-colourful character, and, like many Yorkshire judgments, it is honest, sound and true, for Trueman has done grand service and is a fighter, a warrior, a never-giver-upper. For Yorkshire his bowling partners are good, but not great, and the unfortunate injury-proneness of some of them has subjected him to much overwork. This overwork is not wholly unknown in Test cricket, either, but he meets it with his own sardonic humour. Asked by his skipper to go on a third time under a scorching antipodean sun, he raised a dark, quizzical eyebrow.

'Come on, Freddie, England expects . . .'

'England's always expecting,' growled Freddie. 'No wonder they call her the mother country.'

And with that he went on to bowl his most devastating spell of the day.

(1962)

IMAGINARY INTERVIEWS: THE SEASON'S PROSPECTS
By 'Henry'

1 – THE HON. LIONEL H. TENNYSON

Fortunately, perhaps, the handsome English Captain did not recognise me as 'The Old College Chum' of 'The Cricketer Winter Annual', so the possible introduction of his bootmaker to my tailor did not materialise.

'What, sir, are the prospects of Hampshire this season?' I ventured. 'Boy,' he replied ecstatically, 'we are going to win the Championship. I formulated my scheme for working the oracle while wintering in Switzerland.' 'Yes,' I remarked, 'I saw photographs of you in full chamois-hunting kit in the *Sketch, Tatler, Bystander, Eve, Daily Mail, Daily Mirror, Daily Sketch, Home Chat*, and *Comic Cuts*, to mention only a few.' 'And,' proceeded the Honourable Tennyson (as the very smartest lady novelists would say), 'I clinched the matter at Ciro's the other night while I was sitting out a dance and reading up the laws of the game in a book called *Wisden*, which the MCC have very kindly lent me. But you want to know what my scheme is? Right.'

Then the good-looking scion of a famous house bent forward in his handsome Chippendale chair, so that his full yet perfectly chiselled mouth was in close proximity to my sinister auricular appendage, and whispered, 'Brown, G!' 'Whizz!' I hissed, the suspense proving nerve-wracking and the temptation unbearable. The Pride of the Bournemouth Festival laughed out loud upon observing my plight, and the clever *mot*, and, with a cheery 'There you are, then,' spake as follows: 'George Brown is, as you may be aware, a fine bat, good wicket-keeper, useful bowler, and magnificent field. Moreover, he wears No. 11 boots, and his skin fits perfectly. The point, old Fishhooks, is this: if we play Brown as a batsman-bowler, we have to include Livsey as a 'keeper. Now Livsey, although a very fine stumper, is a poorish bat, and you cannot afford to play poorish bats in a side that will undoubtedly win the Championship. This is where my scheme comes in.

'During the winter months I have had Brown down at the old baronial hall practising bowling at the covered nets there. He has developed the art to such an extent that he can now toss the ball or caber to a great height, whence it falls with marvellous accuracy slap bang on the top of all three, old Ape, thereby causing a mighty crash of ash, as Freddy Wilson would say. While the batsman waits, with knees a-knock, for the ball to descend, Brown calmly walks, via mid-on and square-leg, to the position usually occupied by the wicket-keeper, and there dons a pair of gloves which are ready, and filled with raw meat, against his arrival, together with other articles of protection unnecessary here to specify in detail. In this facile manner he performs the dual role of bowler and stumper. Hence we are able to include another good batsman in the team, and we shall therefore, de facto, if not de jure, vice versa or whatnot, have a side composed of twelve men, to all intents and purposes.'

'Marvellous!' I ejaculated.

'Quite elementary, my dear Watson,' Tennyson replied joyously. Soon afterwards I took my leave of him. As I closed the door behind me and descended the stairs, I heard roars of laughter proceeding from his well-appointed and gracefully decorated study. Yes, a man possessed of so sunny and brilliant a mind will doubtless regain the Ashes for the Old Country before very long. Watch Tennyson!

2 – THE HON. F.S.G. CALTHORPE

'Hello, Henry!' In this cheery manner was I greeted by the Honourable Frederick S. Gough Calthorpe, Captain of Warwickshire, and one of the famous players Lasky – Repton, I mean. I immediately felt at home in the presence of the old Cantab, who had obviously recognised me as a former frequenter of the Pitt (Finsbury Park Empire), so I started on him at once.

'What are your prospects in the County Championships this year?' 'We shall win it,' he replied, 'and with some ease. In fact, so certain am I about it, that it is worth your while to insure on it.' Waving aside my proffered groat, he proceeded: 'You have noted that Bates is being carefully watched in some of the best-informed quarters? – an England bat of the near future. Moreover, Harry Howell will be quite fit once again, and with Jerry Rotherham and myself to put a little of the rough stuff over, we hope to do more than well.'

'But,' I remarked,' 'the Honourable Lionel Tennyson has already informed me that Hampshire are winning the Championship.' 'Poor old Lionel,' laughed Calthorpe, 'he always was an optimist!'

'How about yourself, Freddy – I beg pardon, sir, Mr Calthorpe?' I asked. 'And do you remember dropping Warren Bardsley off me at square-leg in 1912?' The old Jesus and St Catherine's Colleges man chuckled to himself, 'I had quite forgotten that you once masqueraded as a cricketer, Henry.' 'Thanks very much,' I answered, 'and mine will be a whisky and soda.' Whereupon the Honourable Frederick S. Gough Calthorpe gave immediate and further proof that he is a capital fellow.

3 – MR. P.G.H. FENDER

Observing a tall gentleman in what appeared, at a distance, to be an umpire's coat, bowling at the nets, I at once realised that it could only be

P. G. H. FENDER
IN THE ACT OF KNOCKING THE COVER OFF.

(1921)

the Super-Sweater, with Mr Fender attached. I strode towards him, raised my Hope Bros, special hope, and said: 'I believe I am addressing the King of the Oval?' At the same moment the gasworks blew up, so I apprehended I had said the wrong thing. Quickly disguising myself as a gentleman (business, with tall hat, spats, and a cigar with a band on it), I again approached the great hitter.

'Will you kindly tell me, sir, what you consider to be your prospects of carrying off the County Championship this year?' Without a moment's hesitation the Casual goalie replied,'We are going to win it.' 'Then you disagree with both Tennyson and Calthorpe, who are both firmly convinced that their respective teams will prove victorious?' 'Certainly,' replied the Surrey Skipper, 'and have you read my book?' 'I fear not,' I said, 'as even Wisden at five and a kick beats me.'

'Poor fellow,' quoth the popular and enterprising Captain of the leading County South of the Thames, 'but I will tell you why we cannot lose. Jack Hobbs is fit again – he has tested himself against "Twelfth man" of the "Evening News" in a Ping-Pong tournament held at the headquarters of that game in the Strand – Andy Ducat is seeing them well, and Sandham is in great form already. Peach and Struddy have spent the last few weeks shoving the heavy half-penny – roller – and I have thought out a democratic dodge whereby the pros. shall emerge from the amateurs' entrance, and the amateurs from a mud hut at the Vauxhall end – can you beat it?'

'No, sir,' I replied, 'but cannot you find a left-handed bowler in all Surrey?' 'We haven't a professional good enough as yet,' was the ready answer. 'I agree,' I said, 'but why not keep an eye on the amateur talent – you might find one among the clubs?' 'You had better see the Selection Committee about that,' smilingly replied Mr Fender, who had now assumed pads and gloves, and as I walked away he made one beautiful off-drive, two cow shots, played back at a half volley, and carted a good-length ball outside the off stump over his left eyebrow into what remained of the jolly old gasworks.

(1922)

SYDNEY BARNES
By Ian Peebles

In the opinion of his contemporaries Sydney Barnes was the best bowler of their day, and of any other they ever saw. This was also the opinion of elders who saw but did not, on account of their years, play against him. So it was the view of juniors who, also for reasons of age, were without practical experience of him. The degree of unanimity is astonishing. Perhaps I may be allowed to add my modest vote to it on the strength of one occasion when he bowled a few balls by way of demonstration at the age of sixty-seven, a scene to which I shall later return.

Barnes was innovator and inventor as well as a superb performer. No-one before (so far as one can ascertain) or since has been able to utilise his technique although it was logical and simple, for basically it consisted in bowling the leg-break in the least complicated way, which is to say like the off-break, from the front of the hand. Without the elaborate bend and turn of the wrist the ball can be more simply controlled, and bowled at very much greater pace. All this is perfectly clear in theory yet Barnes has had no outstanding imitator, nor successor. Alec Bedser comes nearest with his turn from the leg, but was rather different in general aspect. Once Barnes had perfected the technique of the 'forehand' leg-break he had scope for an extensive variety of refinements. These could be readily disguised, for the position of the hand, palm toward the batsman, did not change; spin swerve and variation of pace coming from the manipulation of the fingers.

It was an infinite joy to the student of bowling as a craft to spend an hour or so in Barnes's company. A cricket ball was the only necessary prop. This he would drop into a firm grip between first and third fingers, the second acting as a clamp over the top, and free to move as an important component in applying the leg spin, in conjunction with the third and little fingers. The off-spinner was delivered as almost every other orthodox practitioner, from the inside top joints of the index finger, supported to some extent by the thumb. As he explained and reminisced the demonstrator's fingers would snap and, as the ball buzzed, the light of battle would flash in those clear, direct eyes.

For Syd Barnes was in fibre and temperament the stuff of champions. Physically he was always absolutely fit, and would not take the field unless he was so. His character was reflected in his imposing presence. He was about six foot two and, when ninety-four years had lopped off a few inches of height and girth, he still retained a proud and tautly upright carriage. If his features were not 'carved from marble' they were moulded of firm flesh, all expressive of determination, and his eye was, as I have said, fierce and direct – to batsmen he must, like General von Kluck, have been possessed of 'a terrifying glance'. But he had a fine pointed humour and, when he smiled, his customarily rather sombre expression was replaced by a particularly lively and attractive twinkle. A streak of humour is an essential ingredient to the enjoyment of cricket and Barnes, although in no sense a flippant man, had this dry, pointed quality, springing from his alert, decisive mind to the end of his days.

Being a perfectionist he was not an easy man. Many are the tales of his fiery reaction to what he regarded as slackness, incompetence or personal slight. Archie MacLaren, also a man of animated spirit, soon found he had caught a tartar as well as discovered a genius. I have always liked, so now repeat, the tale of sponsor and protégé, after a few weeks' personal acquaintance, in Australia. Boarding a very rickety ship for Tasmania, Archie MacLaren's companion observed that, in view of the prevailing storm, she would almost certainly sink. 'Never mind,' replied his captain cheerfully. 'If she does that b——— Barnes will drown with the rest of us.'

With the more understanding Plum Warner there was never a word of dissension. The truth was that, whilst he could not be driven, real leadership brought out all Barnes's loyalty and unquenchable spirit. Sir Pelham not only regarded him as one of the greatest triers in his experience, but as a very engaging man.

My own personal recollections are of a remarkable and delightful companion. I have kept them fresh by often reflecting upon them, and will ever continue to do so. I was introduced to him by Lady Warner whilst playing in a Test match. Perhaps, being yet innocent, I was responsible for the 'leak' that we spent a wonderful hour whilst he had instructed and reminisced. It was a pity that an enterprising sub-editor had captioned the account 'Barnes tells young bowler how he would get Bradman out.' He was furious at being put in this false light, and it took Sir Pelham's advocacy to convince him that I was naïve, but certainly not guilty.

Eight years later I shanghaied him from a Lord's Test match for a Sunday fixture. This was the wine and spirit firm to which I belonged versus the Bartenders' Guild. He exceeded the call of duty by making the speech of the day at the preceding lunch, and standing umpire. It was between the fall of Bartenders' wickets that I had a glimpse of the promised land. The umpire, in uniform coat and trilby hat, skipped up a few springy paces and, with the most beautiful high wheeling action, delivered every variety of 'request item'. It was plain to any discerning eye that here indeed was the best ever.

To these few random thoughts I was about to add RIP. But, on second thoughts, I doubt if this is a very appropriate prayer in this particular case – not if it should happen that any ghostly 'run-stealers flicker to and fro' in the immediate vicinity.

(Spring Annual, 1968)

MIND MY HAT
By Ian Peebles

Some time ago I found myself on a cultural excursion, a lone male in a bus load of females. As we rolled along the ladies conversed animatedly, as ladies are prone to do. I was gently rebuked by my wife and others within earshot for asking, in all innocence, what they talked about now they didn't wear hats any more. They could well have riposted that the all-absorbing subject of headgear seemed to have been transferred to cricketers, with very much less attractive results.

Never before has such a variety of 'adornment' been seen on the field of play. Much is unbecoming and it is a sad turn of events that it should now be required to protect the batsman's head from the bowler, rather than from the sun in the tropics or the elements in England.

The idea of protective headgear, if now more urgent, is not entirely new. When Summers was killed at Lord's in 1870 from a blow on the head the next man in swathed his head in a towel. Pat Hendren, hit (accidentally) on the same ground by 'Lol' Larwood, later produced a three-peaked cap which proved wholly ineffective. About the same time that splendid Hampshire eccentric, George Brown, emerged to face Larwood at Trent Bridge in what looked like a German steel helmet. It later turned out to be a woman's cloche hat.

This is the first era in which cricket headgear has been expressly designed for protection. Originally it was ordinary headgear of everyday wear – but, with the passage of time, it became more emblematic. A picture of a match in 1760 shows the majority of the players in tricorne hats, one of the more becoming masculine fashions. The minority wear what appear to be postillions' caps which are both practical and becoming.

In passing, a collection of similar paintings came up for sale the other day and turned out to be interesting fakes. At one time there was a great demand for pictures of rustic cricket matches, so an enterprising artist would buy a cheap landscape and overpaint his cricket match in the middle of it. The expert pointed out that the figures therein were the same in most of the pictures, differently positioned, but identical down to the same tricorne hat. *Caveat emptor.*

When the new century was still young it seems that the genteel citizen bent on any activity including, no doubt, the consummation of his marriage, donned an exceeding high topper. It was, therefore, natural that the cricketer should do so when he took the field where, to the practice of under and round arm bowling, it offered no obstruction. A group of champions in the 1840s shows 90% toppers, but a sprinkling of

David Copperfield tasselled caps (such as the gals wore when they used to talk about hats).

Later the bowler hat, in white felt, became fashionable and was much in evidence on the lamentably mismanaged occasion when Albert, Prince of Wales, opened the venture for Lord Skelmersdale's XI and made nought. The bowler took years to become a formal hat and, when a cricketing peer turned up at a race meeting sporting one, the same Prince greeted him with 'Goin' rattin', Harris?'

In the Eighties caps had arrived and the bowler hat had become the off-the-field wear of most professionals. The famous Arthur Shrewsbury was very sensitive about his premature and complete baldness. It was said that in the dressing room he would pop a bowler-hatted head into the tails of his cricket shirt and it would emerge at the collar crowned by a Nottingham cap.

Harlequinade

Despite W.G.'s example the cap of the premier club has always been exceedingly rare and it was left to the elegant four panels of the Harlequin cap to become cricket's most famous emblem on the head of Plum Warner. Its most notorious was on Douglas Jardine, at least in Australia. Incidentally, the Harlequin had fallen into disrepute there before Jardine's first visit. That massive man in person and personality, Reg Bettington, had already worn it when playing for his native New South Wales. The Hill reckoned he would look better in the club cap and said so in appropriately colourful terms.

Of all forms of headwear I have tried, the topee on the cricket field evokes the most painful memories. Perhaps we were not very good at them, but through four long months in India I promised myself a place kick from the poop of the homeward bound ship, to rid myself of the damn thing in style.

I now see that there was never any real necessity for a topee in any country and certainly not in the West Indies. Although assured of this by the natives and experts, those two strong individualists, Wilfred Rhodes and George Gunn, insisted on wearing them in the Caribbean in 1930. One disadvantage came to light in Trinidad. When, at Port of Spain, Learie Constantine hit Bill Voce somewhere into the stratosphere, the upward sweep of George's vision from deep square leg was abruptly checked by the brim of his topee on the back of his neck. His solution to this problem was spectacular, not to say dramatic. With his left hand he raised his helmet high in the air while with his right extended like a beggar's bowl he pouched the ball, the whole effect being of a statue commemorating the Relief of Mafeking.

It was an eventful day for George. He was soon involved in a further incident which could scarcely be ascribed to his hat. He had passed the time chatting pleasantly to a gigantic coloured lady sitting on the boundary line. It was in an effort to intercept a hit in her direction that, making good speed for a fifty year-old, he tripped and, falling flat on his face, shot from sight under her voluminous skirts. There was a considerable pause before he reappeared doing a steady breast stroke, to the delight of the lady.

Another victim of a similar obstruction to George's topee shared with him the distinction of being a masterly player of fast bowling. Major R. M. Poore was six feet four and a splendid all-round athlete when he averaged 91 for Hampshire. When later, as General Poore, he heard a weaker vessel express fears of Larwood and body-line bowling, he grew impatient. 'D'ye know what I would do to Larwood?' he demanded, 'I would charge him, sir, charge him'. Whatever the outcome of this manoeuvre it is certain that the General would not have been daunted.

The mishap befell him late in his career when he was leading an MCC side in the West Country, stationed at extra cover, beneath a panama of such dimensions as to be better described as a sombrero. At cover was Fenner, the senior professional, and the bowler was Jim Powell, who spun a crafty leg-break for Middlesex. The lusty striker was thrashing at these with every good intention but little success and the General was quick to foresee the result. 'Depend upon it, Fenner,' said he, 'we shall be gettin' a catch directly.' Seldom has military appreciation been more promptly fulfilled. Next moment the ball, hard driven against the spin, was rapidly climbing to an enormous height and the General sprang into action. This took the form of revolving on his axis at a steady 20 rpm but, beneath the vast periphery of his hat, his view was limited to that of an inside rider of a merry-go-round. Having spun for a considerable dizzy spell, he eventually admitted defeat. 'No good, Fenner,' he cried, 'can't see her.' His neighbour smiled indulgently. 'I don't suppose you can, sir,' said he. 'Long-on caught it half a minute ago.'

(1980)

GRAVELLY NOOK, BUFFET AND CO.
By Alan Gibson

From time to time I make an effort to throw away some of the piles of paper in my study. These efforts are not often useful, partly because something distracts me before I have got very far, partly because I have sudden doubts as to whether I ought to discard some particular item.

Recently, when engaged on this task, I came across an aged shorthand notepad, on which I had inscribed a list of cricketers' centenaries. I presumably took them from *Wisden*, and I gave up the effort fairly soon, because I notice none of the names begins with a later letter in the alphabet than D. I suppose I thought that they might come in useful some day, and bless me, they have, because I am now able to inform you that the following cricketers (whose names begin from A to D) were born in 1880:

Mr H.Z. Baker (Kent)
S. Cadman (Derbyshire)
Mr T.A. Chignell (Hampshire)
Mr E.M. Dowson (Harrow, Cambridge, and Surrey)
Mr L.T. Driffield (Leatherhead, Cambridge, and
Northamptonshire)
Lt Col A.H. Du Boulay (Cheltenham, Kent, and Gloucestershire).

Familiar names

So here they all are in *The Cricketer* a hundred years later. All the names will, of course, be familiar to regular readers. Who can forget the glorious off-drives of Zephaniah Baker (he was always known as 'Z' to his friends, setting a happy precedent for another 'Z' in county cricket a century later)? Who does not remember the dour defence of Tommy Chignell who, so aptly, fulfilled the original meaning of his name, 'Gravelly nook'? (Frustrated bowlers sometimes found other words, and I believe 'Chugging Hell' was at one time a favourite.) Who that has frequented the Cheltenham Festival cannot recall the genial presence of Buffie Du Boulay (close friends called him 'Buffet', in tribute to his French ancestry)?

And now I will tell you some true things about the others in the list for, if you imagine I am going to look those first ones up, and turn them into less interesting characters, you are mistaken. Driffield got his Blue at Cambridge in 1902. Dowson was still up at Cambridge, and so long as they had Dowson it did not seem much to matter who else was in the side. Cadman was a professional, who served Derbyshire faithfully, with constant labour if not exceptional skill. In 1920, when Derbyshire played 18 matches (17 lost, one abandoned) he and Morton were the only men who could make any sort of a game out of it.

That leaves us with Dowson. He was one of cricket's great missed chances, though there were many of them about in those days, amateurs who could not give time to the game, or did not care to. He first played for Harrow at Lord's when he was 15. In that year he bowled 90 five-ball overs, and took eight wickets for 195. Whether a 15-year-old boy should have been allowed to do such a thing is another question. In five matches against Eton, he took 35 wickets, average 21. He also scored 281 runs, average 47. He went on to play four times for Cambridge, and was captain in his last year. In these nine matches at Lord's he was only once on the losing side. He must have been just about the best 15-year-old cricketer to play in such circles until Cowdrey appeared for Tonbridge many years later. Curiously, both lost their bowling early (both were spinners, Dowson slow left-arm, Cowdrey a leg-spinner) but both made compensatory advances in their batting.

Cowdrey's career stretched over many years. Dowson played little first-class cricket after his Cambridge days. He was known as 'Toddles', not that he grew up so very small, but in remembrance of his remarkable boyhood beginning.

He was a cheerful and lively lad, Edward Morice Dowson. He came from the same family as the poet Ernest Dowson, indeed I was once misinformed that they were one and the same chap (but Ernest was born in 1867, and died of dissipation in 1900, though not before writing 'I have been faithful to thee, Cynara, after my fashion'). Edward survived until 1933, died at Ashburton and, when I lived in South Devon 10 years or so later, I would still hear stories about him in cricketing circles.

'Tell England'

Ernest Dowson was a friend of Oscar Wilde, and of the other Yellow Book *avant-garde* writers of the Nineties. He did not share Wilde's sexual inclinations. After Wilde's release from prison, when he was living in France, Wilde met Dowson in a café in Dieppe. Dowson offered to conduct Wilde to a local brothel, in the hope that he would acquire 'a more wholesome taste'. They managed to raise enough cash between them, Dowson manfully volunteering to stand outside. Wilde was a well-known figure, and a crowd quickly gathered. When he came out, 'The first in these ten years,' he said to Dowson, 'and it will be the last.' And then, turning to the crowd, he added, 'But tell it in England, for it will entirely restore my character!'

Well, I seem to have wandered some way from my starting-point, and even finished up with the wrong Dowson. I plead in defence that (a) I did throw that notepad away after all, so you are in no danger of being faced with a similar A-D centenary list in 1981, and (b) it's Christmas.

(1979)

LIFE IN THE UPPER ECHELONS

MEMBERS OF THE UNION:
WHEN NOBBY CLARKE FACED ALF GOVER
By J.J. Warr

Undoubtedly a large number of cricketers share the view that there is in existence a Fast Bowlers Union. It may not be affiliated to the TUC but at least all members are entitled to certain rights and privileges. Not least amongst these is the fact that no fast bowler should physically intimidate another. That is to say that everyone bowling above a certain pace discreetly bowls half-volleys at a fellow member.

The merest glance at cricket history shows that no such sinister conspiracy exists. Before the second war Bill Bowes and Gubby Allen certainly did not observe any set of rules. After the war Edrich bowled bouncers at Lindwall, Tyson bowled them at Miller, and Lindwall hit Tyson on the head at Sydney, uttering the memorable sentiment: 'I shouldn't have done that' as Tyson sank to the ground. Again, in the West Indies Dexter had Hall ducking, weaving and finally diving to earth for cover. In most county seasons feuds have developed too numerous to list and certainly nobody would be so foolhardy as to suggest that Trueman has spent his career bowling well-up to nine, ten, jack.

However, perhaps the most famous example of the brotherhood at loggerheads is the least well-known. In St Ives, in Huntingdonshire, stands a small pub kept by a former England and Northamptonshire fast bowler, Nobby Clark. The walls of that excellent tavern are not decorated with old bats, stumps, or faded score-cards, but they are lined with the pictures of some of Nobby's victims. Batsmen are shown in various agonising postures grasping some part of their anatomy recently struck by a very hard cricket ball. You could be in the out-patients department of any big hospital. From this, one can surmise that quite apart from being a great fast bowler in the sense of wicket-taker, Nobby Clark could also present to the batsmen quite tricky problems of self-preservation.

Well, in 1948 having retired from Northamptonshire, he was invited to turn out for the Minor County of Cambridgeshire. He duly accepted, and his first match was against Bedfordshire at Luton. Alf Gover in that season had visited Luton for a Sunday match and in a generous moment when his resistance was lowered by local hospitality, he agreed to appear for Bedfordshire. (Incidentally, he played twice for them, taking twenty-five wickets in the process.) So the stage was set for the encounter between two great old lions of the fast-bowling fraternity.

Courtesy of Punch

BYSTANDER: 'Good match, old fellow?'. BATSMAN: 'Oh yes, awfully jolly'. BYSTANDER: 'What did you do?'. BATSMAN: 'I had a hover of Jackson; the first ball 'it me on the 'and, and the second 'ad me on the knee; the third was in me eye; and the fourth bowled me out'.

Jackson's 'fearsome pace' was well enough known for Punch to produce this cartoon, the first ever on cricket, in August 1863.

(1984)

On the day Cambridgeshire won the toss and batted first on what proved to be a very rough wicket. Those batsmen not bowled out were laid out. The ball flew about alarmingly but Nobby at number eleven watched the whole scene with equanimity. 'Alf will keep it well pitched up to me,' was the only comment he allowed himself. Eventually he had to bat, and his first stroke was the tentative half-forward prod which had served him so well throughout his cricket career. The ball was short of length, hit a daisy and flicked the lobe of his right ear. At this the whole of the fielding side and the remaining fit members of the batting side burst into uncontrollable laughter. Nobby, like Queen Victoria, was not amused. Indeed, he hurled his bat to the ground and gave the following stern address to the fielding side, 'You are laughing now,' he said, 'but I will fix you, one by one.' It is interesting to speculate what method of extermination other than that on an individual basis passed through his mind. However, he automatically declared the innings closed by storming off the field in the highest of dudgeons.

He beat the umpires out on to the field again and had marked out his run and was pawing at the ground when the two Bedfordshire batsmen entered the arena. The one to take first strike was a small, inoffensive man, well-known for the rather dour quality of his batting. The opening delivery was awesome in velocity and hit the poor fellow plumb on the left ear. He collapsed in a heap with a sympathetic fielding side gathered round him. In the general excitement nobody had noticed a prostrate figure at the bowling end. Nobby, tensed up and forgetting his age, had put so much into the initial onslaught that he had pulled every muscle from his ankle to his head.

It is probably the only time in cricket history that the opening bowler and batsman have been carried off simultaneously from the field of battle. I don't think Alf Gover's union card would have saved him that day – but we shall never know.

(1962)

MY REMINISCENCES
By G.L. Jessop

My second season at the Varsity was a red-letter year for me. In the first place, it was the only one in which I was not more or less crocked. As a Fresher I had the most uncomfortable experience of having to bowl on the hard ground of Fenner's with the nails of my left foot in a state of suspended animation, owing to some thirteen stone of humanity descending with no fairy-like tread upon them. This had happened the previous March, whilst playing centre-forward for Gloucester against Warmley in a Western League game at Gloucester.

In the early autumn of 1897 I accompanied Mr P.F. Warner to America – of which more anon – and on the return voyage met with a sorry experience. I do not often boast, but let me say at once that I hold the belt – gold or otherwise – for the championship as the worst sea traveller of the cricket world. Despite rumours which have reached – horrible word! – me about George Hirst being no slouch in this direction, and regardless of the evidence of my eyes as to the Jam of Navanagar in a later trip, I remain quite undisturbed as to the clear rights of my claim to the title. My unfortunate experience happened when in the throes of *mal de mer*. At such a moment one tries to get rid of everything, even one's blankets – which I did. Unfortunately an iceberg chose that moment to make its appearance, and the sudden lowering of the temperature resulted in awarding me an attack of renal colic from which I did not really recover until the winter of 1898.

From November 1897, until the following Whit-Monday, under the advice of a specialist, I essayed to enact the role of a Nebuchadnezzar. Vegetarianism may be a cure for all the ills which flesh is heir to, but it is wretched stuff to make runs on. Some people it may suit; it certainly did not suit me. For the whole month of May I could get neither runs nor wickets, and it would not have surprised me if I had been dropped from the team in consequence.

The turning-point, however, came upon the Whit Monday at Brighton, whither I had journeyed to assist Gloucestershire. The 'Old Man' was much concerned over my ill success, and resolved to prescribe for me in his own fashion. I forget whether it was Goelet 1889, or Moet 1886, for I have not the prescription by me. Anyway, it had the desired effect, and I bade farewell to vegetarianism for ever.

The following year – 1899 – the year of my captaincy, was also an unfortunate one. Half an hour from the commencement of the Test match at Lord's I wrenched a fibre of my bowling muscle, but taking things easily prior to the Varsity match, was patched up with copious plasters by Sir Anthony Bowlby sufficiently to bowl in that game.

Philadelphian swervers

But there were other things besides immunity from accidents which served to make the year 1897 so memorable to me. First and foremost there were the defeats of Plato and Oxford; and also my first century in first-class cricket, and my first appearance in the Gentlemen and Players matches. It was the Philadelphians who assisted me to achieve the first distinction. Formerly their programme had not been recognised as first-class, but the good show which they had constantly put up on their own wickets against English teams rightly led to the alteration. They were a very good side that year, quite up to average county form in batting, but rather above it on certain wickets in bowling. They were a team of 'swervers', and when the wind was favourable brought off some astonishing performances. Their slow bowler was a genial little fellow named H.P. Baily – 'Parson' Baily he was called. He was what one might term a speculative bowler, and one full of hope. Inclined to 'swing' a little, he always gave the ball plenty of air, and when he had got rid of it his face bore an air of intense expectancy. He was a bowler of the dogged type; one of that kind who are apt to regard one with hurt surprise if one is so rash as to hit a ball in any direction other than that conceived by the bowler as being the proper one.

In his first over to me, one of his deliveries pitched out of the ground at the Pavilion end. He had a hurried consultation with his skipper, Mr George Patterson – a cricketer, by the way, up to our representative match class – at the end of his over, and the next one from that end was not bowled by him. He appeared, however, at the other end an over or two afterwards, and the very first ball disappeared into what used to be called in ancient days a Ladies' Seminary. I saw certain signs of amusement on the faces of his fellow players and learnt the reason afterwards. The 'Parson' had begged to change ends, as he considered that the top one was too short. He never heard the end of it that tour.

This 1897 team was the best of the four of which I was a member. It was strong in every branch, especially in fielding. Excepting for two 'croppers' against Sussex, we won all our matches, again defeating Yorkshire. Our captain, Mr N.F. Druce, was one of the batsmen of the year, and earned a place in the English team which went to Australia in the autumn. Mr Druce goes down in my album of good batsmen without a moment's hesitation. He had all the shots, and it was impossible to pick a flaw in the methods which he employed for their execution. In forcing the ball to leg, more particularly in the direction just wide of mid-on, he may have had equals, but no superiors.

The innings which I like best to remember him by was the one which he played in the opening match against Mr C.I. Thornton's eleven. On that occasion Mr Thornton had brought down an unusually strong bowling side. Besides the three professionals, Hirst, Woodcock, and Alec Hearne, there was a pretty useful amateur performer in the person of Hon. F.S. Jackson. Against this formidable array Mr Druce broke the record for the highest individual score at Fenner's, carrying out his bat for 227. I always quote that knock as one of the finest I ever saw, and one of the few big innings to which one could reasonably apply the word faultless. Had Mr Druce seen fit to continue his first-class cricket to any length of time after he left the Varsity I am convinced that he would have occupied the same position in English cricket as poor Victor Trumper did in Australia. It is given to few to combine brilliancy and safety in so effectual a manner as did the Cambridge captain of 1897.

(1921)

THE PROFESSIONAL CRICKET WIDOW
By Frances Edmonds

The Cricket Widow (Vidua Cricetoris Vulgaris) is a hardy annual, found ubiquitously in our green and pleasant land. It buds in early May, blossoms (depending on weather conditions) in June or July, and fades out towards September. It survives in even the most adverse situations, such as simooms of sweaty socks and jock-straps, and swamps of biologically-soaking, grass-stained cricket whites. On fine days it is occasionally to be seen in clusters, dotted around village cricket grounds. It comes in all shapes and sizes, is variegated in colour, and can often be transplanted into the rugger season with much the same practical and decorative effect.

The Professional Cricket Widow (Vidua Cricetoris Professionalis) is a mutation of the former variety, much tougher and more resilient. It is a relatively recent development, thrives well in England, but far better, intensive research has ascertained, in the Tropics and Antipodes. In this country it is mainly to be found in well-sheltered, sunny spots at all the major botanical beanfeasts, such as Lord's, The Oval, Trent Bridge, Edgbaston, Headingley, etc.

The Professional Cricket Widow boasts some quite astounding characteristics. Though the male of the species might deem the female virtually incapable of putting two and two together with any degree of accuracy, she can nevertheless reel off scores, averages, run-rates, bowling figures and a plethora of other abstruse statistics with the speed and precision of an IBM computer, or a Bill Frindall.

Some of the post-Packer strain (Vidua Multae Pecuniae), however, have developed a most distressing genetic defect, and their passion for figures extends no farther than the joint bank account. (See 'Cricket, Wicket, and Nickit', Cambridge University Press.)

Another quite alarming behavioural defect which is becoming ever more dominant in the Cricket Widow variety generally is a dangerously aggressive and vindictive streak. If Jeremy de St Oswald Nepotismrule-sok breaks a leg skiing, leaving Hubby's position as opening batsman unchallenged, the male of the species will disguise his sincere and immediate reaction of 'WHOOPEE' with some well-tried sportsmanism from the Canons of good Cricketing Behaviour, some unfelt gem such as 'Bad Luck' or 'Hard Lines'.

The Cricket Widow, on the contrary, has a right, nay a conjugal duty, to pontificate on the righteous wrath of the gods, and to point out forcibly that if his grandfather did not own the ground Jeremy would never even have got to first base (or whatever the cricket equivalent may be).

The Professional Cricket Widow, though equally, if not more, vindictive, will be slightly more diplomatic. For a start, few professional cricketers' grandfathers own grounds. She may confine herself to the charitable reflection that, if the professional equivalent of Jeremy had not spent the whole year organising his Benefit (to the indubitable detriment of his game), and raking in all those spondoolicks from the stripes on his shoes, logo on his jumper, and trade-mark on his bat, he would never have had the money to go skiing in the first place. Of course, the male THINKS it, but it takes the female to actually SAY it.

The Professional Cricket Widow serves also as a very useful scapegoat. Since time immemorial, when Adam, the quintessential Man, decided to lay it on Eve, rather than take the rap himself, Woman has been blamed

"I could let you have this nice warm sweater of my husband's—provided, of course, that you're a member of MCC."

(1969)

for everything from the Trojan Wars to the reduction in the Earth's ozone layer. A cricketer with a good woman behind him (how else, dear, can you stab people in the back?) has a perennial excuse for bad form: 'How can the poor blighter concentrate on his game, with a battle-axe like that to go home to?'

Ab contrario, when he is doing well: 'Marvellous what the lad can do, despite the old bag he's got to contend with'.

Super squad

Recently, however, startling almost unbelievable facts have been divulged about Professional Cricket Widows. It is a very closely guarded secret, but a high-ranking official (aren't they all?) from Lord's – has let it slip that the MCC subscriptions are shortly to be increased by 2.5 million per cent (2,500,000 per cent for the mathematicians amongst you). The reason is not, as you will immediately assume, to cover inflation and increased administrative costs. It is, in fact, designed to finance the studies of the eminent Australian Genetic Engineers, Professors Backscoop and Stump.

In their recently published work, collating results of experiments to date, they describe their attempts to produce a Super Test-tube Cricketer. (See 'Super Tests', Melbourne University Press, Profs. Backscoop and Stump.) Fantastic though it may sound, willing Professional Cricket Widows (Vidua Cricetoris Professionalis) have been crossed with incredible hulks of Close Bank Willow (Salix Coerulea) in an effort to produce the Super Squad of the future. In an excerpt from the book, Prof. Stump describes the inception of the incredible undertaking:

'Watching be-helmeted batsmen on TV, I suddenly realised what a dramatic evolutionary step it would be if cricketers could be produced with solid, wooden heads. This would obviate the necessity for all this ugly headgear, and silence the fuss about dangerous bowling. After much genetic research and experimentation, we feel the end is now almost in sight.'

Given the cerebral qualities of some of the professional cricketers around, one may justifiably wonder if Mother Nature has not pipped Profs. Backscoop and Stump at the post. The Professors, however, are undeterred and, bolstered by large contributions from official and unofficial sources, they continue to soldier on into a Brave New World Series.

As Prof. Backscoop argues in the book's final chapter on sponsorship: 'A wooden-headed cricketer is an ideal vehicle for advertising. First, of course, he doesn't ask any questions, which suits both sponsors and the administration. Secondly, the financial pressures won't affect his game, as best quality Salix Coerulea is incapable of any sort of thought process.

Thirdly, the sponsor's logo can quite simply and effectively be carved into the forehead, for maximum TV coverage. And fourth, no more distressing scenes of blood and teeth on the pitch. A bouncer hitting the head would produce the familiar and classical sound of leather on willow. Runs thus scored would, of course, be Head-Byes.'

Yet what of those selfless and anonymous Pioneers of Progress, the Professional Cricket Widows who agreed to participate in these experiments? They, as usual, remain unthanked and unrecognised beyond the boundaries of fame. But, when the first team of England Woodentops brings home the Ashes, there will be a tear in the eye of many a PCW who was left to her own devices for the four months of a winter tour.

(1980)

'STAND UP AND FIGHT' – A TEAM TALK
By Peter Roebuck

Suddenly there was a flash of lightning, tremors slid down everyone's backbone. Our leader arose to speak to his assembled crew. A hush rolled around the room, for our captain is a formidable man. Heads hang low for fear of meeting him eye to eye. Like a Gestapo interrogator his eye strips you naked, revealing all. Moments of horror creep back to mind; that time I had an appalling slog just after the leader had ordererd me to 'get your head down, lad, and keep it down'. It all comes back. Does his roving, bloodshot eye see it?

He stands on the table now, arms spread wide like the start of a Rank International film. He pauses, though he has not yet begun. The hush deepens into gloom. They say evangelical preachers in The South create unfathomable pitches of silence before the haranguing begins.

Our leader glares around him, slowly rolling his eyes. Foam seeps from the corners of his mouth. He sees into the darkest reaches, not a nook or cranny escapes. Shiftless souls who seek solitary seats emerge from the shadows to face the storm.

How shall he begin, we wonder? No, not 'Friends, team, countrymen!' We had that last week. Nor 'Awake, arise or be forever fall'n.' No, that would be too much, even for him. After all it's only the lunch interval and they are 68 for four. Maybe he'll sing 'Stand up and fight, men, fight for your lives'. Surely not, more likely 'Examine yourselves, examine your consciences, examine your performances.' That has a chance, a good Churchillian ring to it and he hasn't used it for a day or two.

How did he view the morning's play, I wonder? His upper lip is curling, obviously he is not happy. Before the game he'd announced that the wicket 'is a line and length wicket', that 'we've got to bowl straight', that 'each of you must face your responsibilities', that 'you must keep your eye on me in the field', that 'if we can get the first five out we're through the beggars', that 'this is the most important game in the club's history' and that 'you've got to be mean'. After this, the boot stamping, the Taunton war dance and then onto the field.

We all make mistakes

I'd done my best; I mean to say, it would have been a helluva catch. I was alert, fit, keen as mustard. So I dropped the ruddy thing, so what? No-one's perfect. I'd like to have seen him catch it. He'd say he'd have caught it 'between the cheeks of his backside'. He probably would have done, too.

And as for that one that slipped through me legs, well I had no chance with that. No chance at all. Bad bounce, rough outfield, spinning ball, fierce hit, no chance. So why did he pucker his eyelids as he swept past me around the room? What about Vic's effort the other day? I mean, it's not for me to criticise, I don't suppose, but it was a pretty tame effort; he could easily have caught it if he'd moved, if he was not so dozy first thing in the morning. Has he forgotten about that? I doubt it; for heavens sake, he still remembers the four overthrows I gave away five years ago. Five years ago! We all make mistakes, these things are unavoidable, aren't they? We're only human, so you've got to be tolerant.

Oh dear. Our leader is not looking terribly tolerant. He's never thought much of namby-pamby, lily-livered liberals. He's glaring at Bill. What's Bill done? Oh, hell yes, now that really was a cock-up. He should have been backing up, he should have stopped the shy at the stumps. Yes, that was pretty poor, I'm bound to admit. He's got every right to bring that one up.

He's opening his lips! My goodness, here we go, over the top lads, all aboard. I bet he speaks well. Not as well as at Chelmsford, maybe. That really was a speech. Lloyd-George, Hamlet, Oscar Wilde, none of 'em could have matched it. Dame Edith Evans perhaps, but then she was a lady and they have an advantage. Just look at Boadicea and Joan of Arc if you doubt it. Chelmsford was a peak, he spoke in an old-fashioned way, varying his voice from boom to hiss, throwing his metaphors into the far recesses of the dingy changing-room. What was it he said?

'Now we are engaged in a great battle, testing whether this county can long endure. We meet on the great battlefield of Chelmsford. The world will note, nor long remember what we do here. It is rather for us to be dedicated to the great task before us, that we here highly resolve that ex-Somerset players shall not have played in vain.'

That's what I call a team talk! No-one knew what on earth he was on about, of course, but it felt impressive; it felt like he meant it (as Macmillan said when Kruschev ranted and raved, banging his fists on the table and shouting – 'I've no idea what he's saying, but he seems to mean it'!)

Is that steam coming out of his ears? Certainly his nostrils are twitching and his neck is reddening. I suppose captains need a bit of fire. Jeeves couldn't inspire a team, nor could Hamlet. Too much low-key wisdom on the one hand, too much dithering on the other. It's no use some nice chap saying, 'Right chaps, we're in a bit of a pickle. The oppo are on top, lads, so let's try jolly hard.' Or even worse, 'Well, chaps, it's a nice day. Things aren't going too well, so let's at least enjoy the sun, the trees and the twittering birds.'

No, that sort of stuff doesn't work. Too weak-kneed; our leader's right really. You feel like those devils in Paradise Lost after our leader has spoken:

'They heard and were abash't, and up they sprang
Upon the wing as men wont to watch on duty, sleeping, found by whom they dread
raise and bestir themselves ere well awake.
Nor did they not perceive the evil plight in which they were, or the fire's powers not feel.'

The pause is over, his throat is moving. He speaks, yes he speaks. 'Umpires in the middle,' yells our 12th man, with the timing of a Groucho Marx. Our leader appears angry, as an actor might if the theatre catches fire just as he is launching into his first 'To be or not to be'. Now we'll never hear that speech. Or maybe we will. At tea-time.

(1982)

2003 – A YORKSHIRE ODYSSEY
By Peter Thompson

The year is 2003. A tepid sun illuminates a Yorkshire landscape scarred by 20 years of civil war. The rubble of once-great landmarks bear cheerless testimony to the intensity of the fighting. Proud families have been riven by the Yorkshire CCC/Geoffrey Boycott conflict; brother set against brother, father against son.

Some of the outsiders snared by the conflict are lucky enough to find sanctuary in York Minster. Others languish in internment camps, fearing what General Ronnie Burnet (Yorkshire Guards) has called the 'final solution' for those who remain 'uncaring, uncommitted'.

The A1 and M62, two great arteries of a once-proud county, carry a human tide of refugees, people so desperate they are willing to start their lives anew in such alien surroundings as Stevenage and Chester. For the womenfolk of God's Great Acres, it is a time of waiting and praying; for dusting down the *Wisdens* and freezing the black pudding in the hope that their Herbert or Wilfred will come marching home.

Burnet is uncompromising. Reform Group members may switch allegiance to the county, thereby escaping internment, but as a penance they must recite, nightly, the Cricketing Gospel According to Lord Hawke, and must keep their heads shaven to allow all loyal Yorkshiremen to pass on the other side of the road.

Scarborough Castle

If the strain becomes too much for Committee members, front-line commanders or leader writers of the *Yorkshire Post*, Burnet has them flown to the Sir Leonard Hutton Home for Loyal Yorkshiremen, in Godalming, Surrey. King Geoffrey, meanwhile, has reached his Scarborough outpost via Lincolnshire, parting the waters of the Humber with one swing of his trusty Slazenger blade. Scarborough Castle has become the headquarters for King Geoffrey's eastern campaign and it is there that the Fifth Yorkshire Lancers are girding themselves for The Last Great Battle.

Their ranks have been boosted by the arrival of Tony Greig's Touring Mercenaries, direct from a special charity performance at police headquarters, Pretoria. There is an air of quiet confidence. In the next few days their ruler will be installed in the Committee Room at Headingley; within a week he will be leading out the New Yorkshire. After that, total domination of world cricket. According to a statement issued through the Lahore branch of the Geoffrey Boycott Appreciation Society, victory will be tempered with mercy, and the current Yorkshire captain, Ghulam Fazal Hamid (Peshawar Primary, Winchester College, Pakistan International Airways and Pudsey) will be allowed to remain on the staff as personal valet and washer of sweat bands to his Highness. But the scent of victory is tainted

The Saint Geoffrey window won't fit? Of course it will; fetch t' bulldozer.

(1984)

by deep sadness. Field Commander D.B. Close, greatest of all war strategists, is gone – killed on the A1 when King Geoffrey called him over ... changed his mind ... sent him back and watched as his staunchest ally took the force of an articulated lorry bound for the fish docks at Grimsby.

Time to get back

King Geoffrey deflected criticism by saying there will always be casualities when you are pressing so hard for victory – 'and besides, old Closey had plenty of time to get back'.

Fifty miles away, the Standard of Yorkshire CCC flies defiantly over the Headingley headquarters. Messages flashed on the electronic scoreboard tell that the price on the head of G. Boycott, professional cricketer, has risen to £2m. In the nets, jovial pipe-smoking Frederick Sewards Trueman – 'call me Patton' – sits atop a Puma tank and announces net practice. The loyal Fred has a personal stake in the conflict; since the war began, his speaking engagements have been reduced from 380 a year to 12. Chris Old, who returned to the colours in the early days of the war, was to have opened up from the Kirkstall Lane end, but reports unfit. 'Pulled a muscle in my trigger finger,' he informs the world's war correspondents.

The Cricket Council has tried for 15 years to find a basis for settlement. In 1994, England's captain, Pieter Van der Merwe (Bloemfontein Secondary Modern, Witwatersrand University, Orange Free State and Devon) led a six-man delegation to Harrogate. The talks broke down when King Geoffrey demanded that all moneys from his War Memoirs (Volumes I to XV) should be used to set up Geoffrey Boycott Memorial Libraries in Leeds, Bradford and Sheffield. Also, he should be allowed to distribute his coaching video, *I Did It My Way*, in all Third World countries where opening batsmen have been seen to get the ball off the square before lunch on the second day.

Further, Dickie Bird should be granted a full pardon for having once taken the armies off for bad light just when the shells were beginning to swing and King Geoffrey's defences were looking vulnerable. The Kissinger Mission of 1998 foundered on the Committee's insistence that any settlement must require Boycott to renounce his claim to the throne, demolish his indoor cricket net, stamp on each set of his contact lenses, forego his diet of honey and gingseng and make himself available for public flogging on the first day of Headingley Test matches. Alternatively, he could settle for exile in Birmingham, Alabama.

No-one could have foreseen that the ceremonial burning of Yorkshire CCC membership cards and Year Books would lead to a civil war. But one thing triggered another . . . the effigy of Raymond Illingworth found hanging beneath the bridge at Knaresborough . . . the Reform Group member discovered wet, hot and dead in the fish fryer at Mrs Chapple's Chippie in High Street, Huddersfield . . . culminating in the taking up of arms at the Battle of Tesco Supermarket (Wakefield branch).

There is a hush across the Broad Acres. They eyes of the world are turned on Ilkley Moor where the two sides will fight The Last Great Battle (lunch 1.15 to 1.50; tea 4.15 to 4.35; a minimum of 20 thrusts in the last hour). Television rights have been bought by Packer's Channel 9 and they have agreed to the BBC taking recorded extracts in return for Huw Wheldon being flown over to give the next Chips Rafferty Memorial Lecture in Wollongong.

King Geoffrey has been at pains to dispel rumours that his war effort has been funded by a new issue of Krugerrands bearing the head of Tony Greig and struck in honour of the Great One's services to the Art of Pitch Inspections. 'Everyone knows my brass is Yorkshire brass,' he tells Prime Minister Mark Thatcher, who is allowed to get off his knees long enough to telephone this information to his Cabinet.

The battle lines are drawn. But wait . . . a message from the Boycott camp says the weather forecast threatens showers and poor light, and the Committee have made no attempt to cover Ilkley Moor . . .

King Geoffrey is demanding an inspection of the terrain before committing his loyal subjects to the Last Great Battle . . .

(1984)

THE RIGHT MAN FOR THE JOB
By Terry Wright

The County needed a new overseas star. Alvin Beamer, their West Indian fast bowler was, by general agreement, past it. Or, at least, his knees were. He had served the county well for eight years. Unlike some other so-called stars, he had troubled the opposition frequently and his own Committee very rarely.

Admittedly, there had been teething problems in the early days. His first practice session had commenced on the edge of the square in typically squally April weather but had ended on the indoor matting wicket. When asked by a local reporter if he preferred grass or matting, Alvin replied politely: 'I don't know, man. I've never smoked matting.'

Fortuitously and coincidentally, the Editor of the Evening Bugle had later that very day been co-opted onto the county committee to fill a vacancy; and the innocent remark was not reported.

BOTHAM ATE FREDDIE STARR'S HAMSTER

LORD LUCAN IN BOTHAM'S CRICKET BAG

IS BOTHAM MARTIN BORMANN?

BINGO £50.000

Neil Bennett

OK, So it ain't Sir Neville Cardus....'

(1986)

'We can't give him a benefit,' said Lord Condominium, the Club President, to Sir Anthony Seneschal, the Chairman. 'A pity. Only eight years, though. A dangerous precedent.' 'Very,' said the suave Sir Anthony, never one to rock the boat by disagreeing with his President. 'Besides,' he added, 'he's done well out of his Test career. He doesn't need a benefit.' Had Alvin felt at that moment a sharp pain in the chest area, it would most probably have been his wallet reacting to the sudden loss of £50,000 or so, tax free. The county committee had still to debate the subject, of course.

Sir Anthony would allow 10 minutes' discussion at the next meeting before, as usual, bringing matters to a close with the familiar words: 'His Lordship's opinion is . . .' Both he and Lord Condominium recognised that the committee would wish to express a view. That the committee themselves were, in theory, but representatives of the members; and that there were thousands of supporters who, though not members, might hold views worth listening to did not occur to either of them even in their worst nightmares. In the old days, there would not even have been a discussion. However, as the President himself frequently observed, the county club must be run democratically – and he would personally hound off the committee anyone who disagreed.

The shortlist

His Lordship and Sir Anthony were meeting, that October evening, to select a new overseas player for the next season from a shortlist drawn up, after extensive research, by Truckle, the Club Secretary. Truckle was in attendance, solely to provide supporting information as required. His opinions were not needed. Lord Condominium possessed an excess of those. Indeed, his brain so teemed with opinions that it had little room left for any facts to support them. In any case, his Lordship found that, when facts did intrude, they signally failed to support his opinions. Consequently, he chose to ignore them whenever possible.

'Perhaps,' said Lord Condominium, easing his massive frame into the imposing chair at the head of the committee room table, 'you could go through the names on your list, Truckle.' 'Certainly, your Lordship,' said

Truckle, a slight, bespectacled man. Previously his Lordship's personal assistant, he sometimes felt that, since taking up his present post three years previously, his role had changed but little. It was, for a born sycophant, a comforting feeling.

'The first candidate,' went on Truckle, leather-patched elbows on the table as he peered at his papers, 'is Curmudgeon, the Australian fast bowler. A typically combative antipodean, your Lordship.' His Lordship's slightly piggy eyes narrowed slightly and he took an extra-hard puff on his Grade-size cigar. 'Is he the one who had the fracas with the Pakistani chappie, what's his name, Popandi?' 'Miandad, I think you mean, your Lordship,' said Truckle tactfully. 'No, that, I believe, was Mr Lillee.' 'Pity,' said Lord Condominium. 'If ever a chap needed putting in his place it's that little upstart.' 'I think,' said Sir Anthony, reaching for the bottle of vintage port thoughtfully placed on the table by Truckle, 'that Curmudgeon is the – er – gentleman involved in the Sheffield Shield riot last year. You remember, your Lordship, when the crowd invaded the pitch, realised they were outnumbered and fled. Curmudgeon was the one responsible for losing a stump.'

'Yes,' said Truckle, 'that's true, your Lordship. But it was recovered later when the spectator concerned had been successfully operated on.' 'I think I've heard enough,' said his Lordship grimly. 'Next candidate, Truckle.' 'There's Van der Blanck, the South African all-rounder. An outstanding talent, your Lordship.' 'There could be trouble, your Lordship, from the anti-apartheid lobby,' said Sir Anthony, anxiously fingering his I Zingari tie, 'That's true,' said his Lordship with a worried frown.

'Oh, no, your Lordship,' said Truckle. 'He's very liberally minded. He's joined a non-white club, publicly denounced apartheid and signed a petition for the release of Nelson Mandela.' 'Has he, indeed,' said his Lordship, his normally pink complexion deepening to that of a new ball. 'Sounds a dangerously radical troublemaker to me. What do you think, Seneschal?' 'Definitely, your Lordship,' said the obsequious Sir Anthony. 'Next, please, Truckle. And tell us the bad news as well as the good.' 'Well, sir,' said the unfortunate Truckle, scanning his rapidly diminishing list, 'what about Lance Lickerish. A fine fast bowler.' He paused. Lord Condominium fixed him with a fierce stare, his cigar poised in mid-air.

'A pity,' stammered Truckle, 'about the topless model, the groundsman's horse and the frogman's suit. Next, your Lordship?'

'Next!' snapped his Lordship, his face a delicate shade of Blofeld puce. 'Well,' said Truckle, perspiring visibly and malodorously, 'there's Peter Rast. A delicate strokemaker, if ever there was one. Averages 43.17 in Tests. No trouble with violence or women, either, your Lordship. Mind you . . .'

His voice trailed away and he looked down at his papers to avoid Lord Condominium's steely gaze. 'Well?' said his Lordship, taking his glass of port from his lips and leaning forwards. 'Well, nothing, really. Even Test cricketers have to visit public lavatories sometimes. Maybe he did have en suite facilities in his hotel room; and maybe an hour and a half is rather a long time to stay there. But who are we to inquire into such personal matters? Besides, I don't think he chose a very good defence lawyer.' 'Quite,' said his Lordship, icily. 'There's more than enough of that sort of thing going on these days. Not married yourself, are you, Truckle?'

'No, your Lordship,' said Truckle hastily, in a slightly deeper voice than normal. 'But I do have a sort of understanding with Miss Ratsbane, the Catering Manageress.'

Ludicrous

'No doubt,' interjected Sir Anthony impatiently. 'Have you no more names? This is becoming ludicrous and a complete waste of time.'

'Well,' said Truckle in some desperation, 'there is Patrick Paragon, the young New Zealander.'

'Any scandals?' asked his Lordship, wiping the excess port from his moustache with his MCC handkerchief.

'No,' replied Truckle, brightening visibly, 'nothing that I can discover. No sexual abnormalities. He's happily married with a baby son. He's even-tempered, kind to animals, does spare-time charity work for old people and has no interest in politics, except for a slight right-wing bias.'

'Excellent!' said his Lordship, rising from his seat. 'Is he available?'

'Oh, yes,' said Truckle. 'He would come for £15,000 a year.'

'Right,' said Lord Condominium, moving towards the door, 'offer him £10,000 with a guaranteed rise in mid-season. If we can't afford the increase at the time, I can always tell him you're an incompetent idiot who made a mistake.'

'Certainly, your Lordship,' said a most relieved Truckle, gathering his papers together. 'I'll do it at once, so we can announce it to the press.' Sir Anthony followed his Lordship to the door and helped him into his overcoat. Lord Condominium took his umbrella from the stand, opened the door and glanced out into the gloom of a foggy October evening. He turned back again to Truckle, who was busily wiping port stains off the polished surface of the committee room table. 'Very pleased with your contribution, Truckle. I'm certain this chap Parapet, or whatever his name is, will be exactly the right man for the job. Another step forward for the old county, eh? By the way, not important, but just to satisfy my curiosity, what is he, a batter or a bowler?'

(1988)

CLUB & VILLAGE

SUMMER RABBIT
By Dennis Castle

Snelling is always first at the club on a Saturday. If wickets are pitched at two-thirty, he is there at one, pipe in mouth, studying the twenty-two yards with meticulous care, testing with thumb and toe. He has unloaded our long brown bags from his car, he has also managed to give a lift to three young members.

When changed for the game, the colours of his blazer, cap and V of his sweater are identical. He knows no divided loyalties, he has but one club. His boots are always newly-whitened – and no blanco stains the leather soles . . . He greets the opposing team as an old friend.

Snelling calls his captain 'skipper' both in the dressing-room and on the field. He studies the posted batting order assiduously, although he has been number eleven since 1938. He doesn't bowl. Regularly he lends his immaculate pads and gloves to the always ill-equipped second wicket down . . . then loads himself with treacherous, finger-chewing deck-chairs which he carefully adjusts along the pavilion rails . . . he has a greeting for all the ladies, a solicitous inquiry after their kiddies . . . he lends the scorer a pencil and makes a promise to the club 'drunk' to give him a lift home that night . . .

If Harry is late, Snelling will umpire for a while. Highly efficient stuff it is, too, with correct signalling and special attention to the batsmen's guards which he checks every other over. He crouches behind the stumps purposefully, head low to watch for 'no-balls!' . . . and he gives out his team-mates fearlessly with, if anything, a bias in favour of the visiting team.

Should he bat at all, his innings is brief. Yet he takes middle-and-leg like a Test player, using a bail to make his mark. With narrowed eyes he

'Nice of you to turn out for us Percy
—deep fine leg and stay there, lunch is
at one-thirty.'

(1963)

surveys the field he will never penetrate. His stumps are spread-eagled . . . he cries: 'Oh, well bowled, sir!' as he waddles away. Once in the pavilion he starts to collect the tea money . . .

In the field the ball bumps past him. You can see him pray that it will go for four. But it stops a yard short. He turns and chases it . . . fat and floundering . . . he groans as he stoops to pick the ball up . . . he throws it in . . . then runs in, picks it up and throws it in again . . . they have run five . . .

And in the evening he buys most of the beer, talks authoritatively on all points of the game, goes into detail on the brilliance of the ball which dismissed him . . .

But, once, just after the war, he made thirty not out against the MCC. He's such a damn bore about it . . .

(1961)

WHERE'S THAT BAIL!

Mr A. Sherring, an enthusiastic follower of cricket for more than fifty years, has sent me the following amusing incident. He writes:

The batsmen were attempting a short run; a fieldsman stopped the ball, threw in hard and hit the wicket, too late, however, to get the batsman out. The ball which was thrown in displaced the bails, one of which completely vanished. For a minute or so the game was held up while the whole team explored the area around the wicket, looking for the lost bail. It could not be found, and a fresh bail being brought from the pavilion the game then proceeded.

About a quarter of an hour afterwards the lost bail was discovered by the wicket-keeper in the seat of his trousers! When the bail flew from the wicket it had lodged in the 'keeper's waist-band, unfelt by him, and by reason of his subsequent activities had eventually found a resting place lower down. The 'keeper extracted the bail from its singular hiding place, and handed it surreptitiously to the umpire. The incident was a startling and hilarious addition to a very thrilling match between Ferguslie and Kelburne, the two famous rival locals teams in the town of Paisley.

(Extract from 'Notes and Comments', 1932)

THE VILLAGE CAPTAIN (*Loquitur*)
By H. D. Owen Brown

I'm not a playing member of the blinking Zingari,
And my cricket ain't exactly what they want for MCC
But on Saturdays in summer you can bet that I'll be seen
In a purple shirt and braces playing on the village green.

I'm not exactly Parkin, and you wouldn't think me Hitch.
I bowl 'em mostly on the leg, and nearly all full-pitch.
But I'm a dangerous bowler – yes, they reckon that a cert.
For I often gets a wicket when the man retires hurt.

I'm not a blooming Sandham, and I ain't exactly Hobbs,
And a straight one always gets me, be it overhand or lobs.
I ain't a budding Jessop, nor a Warner, nor a Hirst,
But I always gets an innings, for I always goes in first.

I'm not a stumping Strudwick, nor a Chapman, nor a Brown,
And if a catch comes to me, you can bet I'll put it down.
And still I go on playing, though I'm over sixty-nine,
For, to tell the truth, I'm captain, 'cos the village green is mine!

(Annual, 1922–23)

ADJUSTMENT OF STATUS
By Charles Rose

It's a beautiful day – sun beaming, larks atrill, children laughing. Our Skipper comes out of the pavilion, a screwed-up bit of fag packet in his hand. He approaches the old school desk parked outside and the clerical spinster who so neatly makes our scorebook balance. I sidle up unobtrusively and lean against a chair, nonchalantly watching a couple of kids hammering midget stumps into the ground. But my ears are flapping like loose sails in a high wind. It's the batting order.

'Blenkinsop, number one,' he says.

(1987)

Fair enough, I reckon. I don't mind opening with Bertie, though he can be a mite impulsive in his calling. Gets over-excited and sees two where there's only a single.

Our visitors haven't got much more than a pair of mild old trundlers, so there's 50 runs apiece for the first pair. Besides, at number two, I'll have a chance to take a squint at any nastigoolies lurking about in the wicket. I don't like being taken by surprise.

'Smith, number two.'

Smith? Is this wise? Oh well, he won't last long, so it comes to the same thing.

'Anderson, number three.'

Tsk, Tsk! I fully realise the lad is promising, but you can't dismiss my wealth of experience willynilly. Dammit, we do want to win the game. Ah, wait a bit, this gives me the Bradman slot. Smart thinking, Skipper. The opposition get a couple of quick wickets and then their hopes are cruelly dashed when the skill arrives.

'Speakman, number four.'

Yes, yes, I see. Same idea. I stroll in at three wickets down, just as the spinners come on. Loplolly for my devastating drives. Yes, it's a comfort-able place. Considerate

'Number five . . .' He hesitates. The scorer's sharpened medium HB hangs poised a year or so. Come along, old chap, you know my name backwards! He peers at his scribbled list. 'Can't read my own . . . oh, that's it, Brown.'

Hell's teeth! Is he serious?

'Number six . . .'

All right, so they'll soon be skittled out. Serves them right. Then I suppose I'll have to steady the boat. Hmph! If that's the way you want it.

'Number six, Capel.'

This is crazy! He's got me down to go in at number seven. Full many a flower may well be born to blush unseen, but nobody expects me to come trailing along half an hour after the match has got under way.

'Number seven, Bradley.'

Zounds! Does that man know I'm playing today? Cough! Better still, knock something over! Remind him you're here! Startled look, astonished cry. Oh my goodness! Confusion, apologies, big beam, looks of relief all round and we write the whole list out again with a significant insertion at number one.

The chump hasn't noticed. Aren't I big enough to see now I'm standing on his foot?

'Number eight, Brockman.'

This is bloody outrageous! I'm at number nine? He who amassed an effortless eight only last week. And who would have done the same the week before if that ass Blenkinsop hadn't assumed we were both Olympic sprinters!

'Number nine, Leonard.'

Oh, of course! That's right, promote yourself! Why not? The whole thing's an utter farce anyway. Can't someone stop those blasted brats from making all that row? And they can turn those twittering birds off as soon as they like.

'Number ten, Kelderis.'

Who cares now? The universe lies in ruins. Meaningless ruins!

'Oh yes, our friend here at number eleven.'

The humiliation! I turn on my heel and stride away, my back a rigid reproach of silent disdain – if anyone happens to notice. Footsteps behind. A clawing paw flops on to my shoulder. I stop and stare polite icicles into his half-witted face.

'Hope you don't mind dropping down the order a bit?'

A bit! Any further and I'd have been in Vladivostock. I say nothing, however. One doesn't.

'Wanted to try a few experiments.'

Lame, pathetically lame! He thinks I'm past it. Ha! But I merely reply, 'Quite.' He is withered by my urbane courtesy.

'Besides . . .' There's an attempt at a manly smile, but it smirks into oily hypocrisy. What feeble excuse now? ' . . . I want you to open the bowling later. Which end do you fancy?'

Open the bowling? Why didn't the cuckoo say? What a splendid fellow he is! How full of human understanding and the deepest knowledge of the game!

I glance down modestly at my boots. 'Yes, well, yes, all right. Do what I can.' Old and far-seeing eyes sweep the stretch of turf. I sniff the smell of battle. 'The slope towards the trees should help the odd off-break, don't you think?'

'I'm sure it will. Work out what field you'd like. I knew I could rely on you.' A firm hand smites my shoulder and our noble leader is off about his many duties.

Open the bowling! It must be years since . . . well, never mind. Larks exalt in the clearest of skies. Darling infants play around my feet.

Wait till I tell them about this in the office on Monday! Round about coffee time should be decisive. A casual mention. That'll shake those young whippersnappers who think they've invented energy. Open the bowling, eh? I should just think I will!

(1981)

THE DAY I SAID I'D DO THE SCORING
By Julia Jennings

The faith behind the plea is as misguided as touching: 'They haven't got an umpire, so . . . would you mind frightfully doing the scorebook?' True, at the age of 14 or so and making a regular job of it, one knew the ropes; now they are pretty frayed from long disuse. One can hardly refuse, though, even if the weather forecast did read like an ad. for Ambre Solaire this morning, prompting one to bring along a supply of the same, together with a rug and (whisper it not in Gath) a good book.

This happens, I suppose, two or three times a season. Always away. And being the sort of side that can't provide an umpire, they can't produce a scorer either. I am alone, in some corner of a foreign field – the corner farthest away from the pavilion.

Our own ground, now, that has everything. There's the box, slap beside the pavilion for running the odd personal errand ('Any tea going?') between their comings-in and their goings-out; and close enough to see exactly what's going on out there and, if necessary, hail the nearest fielder for details of 'bowler's name' and 'who was that catch by?' And there are anything up to nine batsmen sitting around; at least one of whom is knowledgeable enough to inform one that the batting-order has been changed all of a sudden. And enough sun gets in to make the Ambre Solaire worth its while.

Above all, there is the small boy – bursting to change the scoreboard, even if it means balancing on a chair balanced on a bench. 'Shall I put the runs one by one?' he asks, with ten minutes to play and 59 to make.

But no small boy will show up here, so far from home base, and even if a couple of strolling members of the batting side do pass by (unlikely, in this heat) they won't know anything about batting-orders. Either they'll be already out, or have been pre-cast as 10 and 11 and will be mildly surprised if they have to bat at all: much they will care if 6 and 8 have been swapped at the last moment.

The box seems to be at least 15 yards from long-on – a section of boundary that apparently fielders simply don't patrol, ever. I did ask their captain to yell across to me his bowlers' names and so on, and of course he said he would, and of course he won't.

The 'Will you score?' came, inevitably, about three minutes before the start of play. I gathered our book and theirs (they'll be lucky); a book of the Laws, property of our Arthur who's to do their umpiring for them; his little box of rubbers, nicely sharpened pencils and clips for holding the Laws open at that useful page of diagrams of umpires' signals; my bag and spectacles and drink; and the key to the box. In the course of the long walk halfway round the pitch I also collect two watches and a wallet, from three total strangers.

The door is at the back of the box, via a bed of nettles and a flight of muddy steps; and the lock sticks. By the time I'm in and settled three balls have been bowled and for all I know they may have been scored off. But they are batting, and they haven't given the best possible impression, facility-wise. Three dots.

'Let's have the cress sandwiches finer and deeper, and the rock cakes squarer. . . .'

(1981)

99

End of first over, and a chance to look around for the telegraph. They can hardly expect the runs to go up as they come, but presumably they will eventually get up to 10 and have a right to know about it.

Zeus (hurler of thunderbolts, and so surely the patron of this most pagan of all games) help me! *Fifteen* strips of canvas! And more than fifteen square holes, and a *stack* of numbered squares. The three strips in the centre are, I assume, for the total. The three on each side, each with a single hole-and-strip above, must be for the current batsmen. Here, I think, is where I can now show one wicket and here batsman two's 0 runs.

No time for a recce — second over is half-way through and they've reached 10. I yank the most central strip until an '0' shows against the light and get a rather torn '1' showing beside it. As for batsmen one and three, they can wait until they're out before their scores go up — this box was designed for two men and a fast-moving boy.

Over four brings them to 20: I signal the fact (I think) and while batsman three, top-heavy with pride at still being in, is having the sight-screen moved, I have just time to check the lay-out from out front. The total shown is 002. Back through the nettles, up the steps, sight-screen still not placed to three's satisfaction so time to correct the score and muse on the purpose of all the little holes that make the front of the box look rather like the negative of a crossword puzzle. Number of overs bowled? Fielder's number? Lord's hath not anything to show more fair, and Canterbury by comparison is pretty primitive.

End of over five, and I wish I'd been taught a little more arithmetic and wasted less time on geometry and Calculus. Already my figures don't add up. By the time they do, they have been deprived of one or two runs — but it's our bowlers I shall be seeing every weekend for the rest of the season.

It rains. (Glad I didn't waste the Ambre Solaire.) The captains and the umpires huddle. *Exeunt omnes.* I gather our book and theirs (the latter blank); Arthur's book of Laws and his useful little box of pencils and rubbers and clips; my bag and spectacles and empty glass; the key to the box; two watches and a wallet; stand in the rain until the key finally turns, and plod back towards the pavilion. Halfway there the rain stops and they all come out again.

My name appears at the foot of the page: I dislike anonymous crimes, and anyway *our* innings was pretty-well accurately kept — that's to say, we won. *Their* name is at the foot of my memory, ready to float to the surface when we play them again next year. The game will be away again — this fixture always is — and I shall be away too. At Lord's, where *both* sides have an umpire from the start and *nobody* will ask me to do the scoring.

(Spring Annual, 1969)

ONE OF LIFE'S TAILENDERS
By Barry Norman

As I may have said before, the only thing that prevented me from opening the batting for England and spinning Australia to defeat on countless occasions was a cruel accident of fate.

But for that there is simply no knowing what I might have achieved. Bradman's overall average of 99.96 is something I'd have settled for only in one of those lean seasons that afflict all great Test batsmen from time to time; while Jim Laker's 19 wickets in a match, though a fair performance to be sure, is one that I would confidently have expected to emulate several times and surpass at least once in my long and breathtaking career.

Could I have been, I sometimes ask myself wistfully as I think of the record books that will, alas, never now bear my name, the first to reach 10,000 runs in Tests? *And* the first to 500 wickets? The answer to both comes to me swift and clear: certainly.

So what was this sad accident that dashed such high expectations? Quite simply the fact that I was born without any discernible talent for the game whatsoever.

When in that Great Pavilion in the Sky down whose steps we all marched to polite applause to take our guard at the wicket of life and to which we must all return when our innings is over, when up there they were handing out the cricketing ability I only just got in ahead of the halt and the blind.

I protested, of course.

'Hang about,' I said to the Lords of Creation (Test and County Cricket Division), 'hang about, there's been some mistake.'

They'd just handed me this tatty little parcel marked 'Cricketing Gifts'. A pathetic thing, it was, hardly big enough to fill one's box. I couldn't believe my eyes.

'Oh dear,' they said, 'we've got another one here, reckons he ought to be W.G. all over again.' And to me they said, sighing in a resigned sort of way: 'All right, squire, if you insist. We'll check the score sheet again.'

So they did and they shook their heads and said: 'Just as we thought. There's no mistake. That's all you get.'

'No, wait,' I said. 'I can't build an entire career around this rotten lot.'

And they looked at my little parcel of gifts and said: 'You're not wrong there, squire. Still, if you use 'em all up at once you might at least have one decent game to look back on at the end of your life.'

Way up at the head of the queue a burly young fellow was staggering away so burdened with cricketing ability that it was a wonder he could walk straight. 'Look here,' I said. 'This simply isn't fair. Compare what you've given that bloke with what you've given me. Can't I have some of his talent? He won't miss it.'

They looked at the young fellow in question and shook their heads emphatically. 'No way, squire,' they said. 'We're expecting rather a lot from that one. Of course, he won't go into bat in life until some time after you but take our tip and keep an eye out for him. We're thinking of calling him Ian Botham.'

And that was that, really. There was no arguing with them. Nothing I could do except take my place as one of life's tailenders and fifth-change bowlers – the kind Derek Ufton brings on in Lord's Taverners games when the opposition's scoring rate has got bogged down a bit.

At this point you might well exclaim: 'Hold on. What are you complaining about? At least you've played with first-class cricketers.' And this is strictly true.

By craftily stretching my limited gifts thinner than knicker elastic and combining them with the ersatz celebrity that comes to all who appear often enough on TV (what I call the 'Look, there goes whatsisname' syndrome) I did manage to sneak into the Taverners.

Indeed, I have stood in the slips alongside Phil Sharpe, borrowed Jack Robertson's bat and Reg Simpson's pads and had Colin Cowdrey dropped in the deep by an actor preening himself in front of his admirers.

One Sunday, using up all the fielding ability at my disposal, I held an amazing running, diving, right-handed catch to dismiss Richard Gilliat in his own benefit game on the Southampton county ground. I've played at The Oval with Bobby Simpson and Ollie Milburn and scored one not out. And once I very nearly ran out John Snow – not that it would have been much of a feat really, since he was my batting partner at the time.

But, oh yes, I have my memories. And they've all been very nice to me, the great ones with whom I've played. Yet it's not the same, standing there in the shadow of heroes and hearing people say: 'Who's that with John Edrich and Brian Close?'

Sometimes when I contemplate what might have been if only I'd been nearer the front at the Great Pavilion in the Sky, I think with a sense of loss of the mighty cricketer who lurks inside me trying vainly to get out.

And then I think: if ever we get a second innings in life, even if it's only to follow-on, I won't take any chances. I'll not only be at the front of the queue next time – I'll be at the ground, clutching my sandwiches, hours before they even open the gates.

(1982)

CRICKET AND CAPER SAUCE
By Laurance Woodhouse

The question has often been put to me, 'What was the jolliest match you ever played in?' My answer, I am bound to say, has varied from time to time. There have been times when one's small personal triumphs have led one to think that such-and-such a match was the 'best ever'. Then, again, one remembers a desperately tight finish, and that match 'beat the band.' One remembers years of country-house cricket at Patshull Park, when Lord Dartmouth (then Lord Lewisham) gave one plenty of the very best kind of sporting cricket, especially when we attacked the house-party from Weston Park, Lord Bradford's country house, with the redoubtable 'Willie' Bridgeman in command, and the Goslings and the Bromley-Martins in his team. These were great days and great names.

But now 'in the sere and yellow', here is my considered decision of the 'jolliest match' I ever played. It was in a little village in Devonshire. A village situated seven miles from any railway station. A village where many of the inhabitants have never travelled in a railway train. It was patriarchally ruled by 'The Squire', and vice-regally governed by the vicar and the leading farmer, incidentally a churchwarden. Both vice-roys were sportsmen of the very best type, and that despot, 'The Squire', · looked on their little weakness in this respect with indulgence, and from a well-filled purse supplied the sinews of war to keep the lads of the village happily employed in their leisure time. Arrives the month of April, and with it a certain liveliness among the younger men of this small village. The squire has again granted permission to use a certain meadow for cricket purposes. He has also suggested to a couple of his young gardeners that they had better put in a bit of work on that meadow, under the direction of the vicar, an old and experienced cricketer. Furthermore, the carpenter, the grocer, the blacksmith, and, indeed,

'. . . head well over the ball, bat and pad together . . .'

all the good fellows of the village, as soon as their day's work is finished, repair to the meadow and get to work on the pitch. Then, a fortnight before the first Saturday in May, appears the notice in the post-office window, 'Married v Single, on Saturday, May 3.'

Then, indeed, life is all of a bustle in that village. The vicar captains the Married, the village schoolmaster the Single. Both are busy getting together the best possible teams, for (never let it be heard above a whisper in these days of pure amateurism) there is a wager on the match! The losers are to pay for a boiled leg of mutton supper, with caper sauce and accompanying vegetables, ditto ale, at the local inn. And, mind you, no one must play but members of the club (sub. 1s a year, and 3d subscription to expenses for all 'out' matches).

The great day arrives. The vicar has a strong team, both his church-wardens and the local miller, who 'hasn't seen his boots for years', are playing; the schoolmaster has whipped up a promising lot of lads about eighteen years old, for they marry young in the country. The whole village goes gala. The little shops all shut up. Everyone crowds to the cricket field – even the policeman finds that 'duty' lies that way, and a stranger could go through every house that day; indeed, a 'Deserted Village'.

Both sides strive desperately; Virgil's boat crews never knew what a *real* struggle was. The Single are afraid of, 'Fancy being beaten by a passel of granfers!' The Married dread the jibe, 'You'm better fitted for a bath-chair!' if they lose. Then, in the evening, with the vicar in the chair, and the schoolmaster in the vice-chair, what a splendid supper and what splendid appetites to tackle it with! The teams sit down, master and man sitting side by side, and all is good cheer. 'The King!' cries the vicar, and the National Anthem is sung heartily and well, for since the vicar is a cricketer most of the cricketers are in the choir. Everybody at that table has to sing a song or tell a story, otherwise he is fined for the benefit of the cricket club. Curious old folk-songs are sung, and then comes 'Good-night!' and the losers have to stand the supper. The bill comes to eleven shillings, or, as the landlord said, 'A tanner a nob.' Keep it a secret, the Squire always footed the bill, and the eleven shillings went to cricket club funds.

But I can remember no jollier matches, and no more sporting ones from every point of view.

(1922)

LORD DUNSANY'S WONDERFUL TRICK
By E.J. Metcalfe

Of all my tours, I think the Free Foresters Irish tours were the most enjoyable. We used to go first to Belfast and by motor to the late Lord Dunleath's place in Co. Down, 'Ballywalter'. We usually arrived on Sunday, mid-day, and there found besides our host and hostess and the family, eleven of the home side collected by the late Teddy Mulholland, alas, killed early in the war, and no less than 22 girls in the house party, making about 50 all told, a truly marvellous performance, sitting down 50 to each meal, and everything working like clockwork, thanks to Lady Dunleath, who arranged everything, and there never was the smallest hitch.

But it was strenuous work. Breakfast at 9, a round of golf on their private nine-hole course, cricket at 11.30 to 6. Lawn tennis till 8. Dinner at 8.30. Dancing after, till one – as there were 22 girls in the house, it was imperative that my side should not only be able to play cricket, but also to dance. Unfortunately, on one occasion, two of my side, an Eton master, and young Carol, did not dance; unknown to me they went into the huge drawing room, which was turned into a dormitory for about eight of the home side, and made apple-pie beds, and also tied up and mixed all their pyjamas.

We were always sent off to bed at one o'clock sharp, and therefore at that hour, the occupants of the drawing room found out their troubles. You could hardly expect them not to make reprisals, and they marched to our dormitory, which was over the stables. In they came, most of them well over six feet; they not only conquered us, but utterly destroyed us. They had, however, decided that the Eton master was the sole culprit; he fought hard but was overpowered. His pyjamas, I fear, were torn to ribbons, his hands and feet tied, and he was frog marched through the garden to the pond, with Carol Lyttelton, his fellow culprit, leading the march solemnly with two lighted candles. When there, he was untied, and duly submerged. The whole thing was done very quickly, almost without a sound. What, therefore, was our astonishment to find that the young ladies knew all about it. On enquiry, we found there was nothing strange about this, it was a lovely August night, with a harvest moon, and the ladies were enjoying it leaning out of their window. Consequently, unknown to us they saw the procession. When we told the culprit he was much abashed, as I regret to say he had no clothes on.

The last night of the tour was always very gay, and I found it was the custom for the Captain to propose the health of the host and hostess.

This was a most difficult performance, because, candidly, no-one was listening to a single word, all being far too well engaged, because on the last evening the ladies had the privilege of asking anyone they liked to take them into dinner, and by this time things had generally got pretty well sorted out.

To the Castle

From this hospitable mansion we motored next morning to play the North of Ireland at Belfast, but I fear the events of the previous few days, and the thoughts of what they had left behind them, produced a depression on the side, and I cannot remember ever being very successful in this match. From there we went to Dunsany Castle. It would indeed be difficult to explain, in writing, what a wonderful host Lord Dunsany was, very much assisted by Lady Dunsany. The things he did to entertain us would fill a book, he has written many himself and his drawings are extremely good, besides which he is a very good shot with gun and rifle, and an all round sportsman.

The first time I went there as skipper, he took me round the ground where he had stumps placed at intervals, and the boundaries, instead of counting four, were two past one stump, three past another, and so on. I had to get the services of our umpire to take careful note as it was altogether beyond me. The scoreboard in the event of anyone not scoring was marked with an animal representing a duck instead of the usual 0. When fielding he would come on the ground in an ordinary cap, but sometimes in the middle of an over, when he was bowling, he sent for an enormous felt hat. He said it gave him inspiration and he frequently got a wicket thereby. I am not surprised for the hat was truly a terrible affair. In the evening after an excellent dinner he always had some amazing entertainment for us. One night he produced two large horse pistols, from which he fired lighted candles. He challenged anyone on my side to a duel at 20 yards, but generously offered his opponent three shots before he himself fired, each to have 12 shots; if one of the candles came sufficiently close to make the opponent duck, the battle was over. A Cambridge boy took the job on, and duly fired his three shots which went quite in the wrong direction, much to the danger of the house and the ladies, then started a fusilade from Dunsany and his fourth shot would certainly have hit the Cantab had he not dived.

All blacked up

Another evening he performed his wonderful trick. I have never seen a better, and although I have seen him do it many times, I have never known it to fail. Dunsany goes out of the room and we then have to pick on one of the people present, whose name is written on a piece of paper which is carefully folded. Dunsany is then recalled, and given the paper. He proceeds to burn same in the shovel, until it is all ash, he then bares his arm and rubs the ash on the skin which immediately shows the name of the person chosen, and it is always correct. The third time I saw him do the trick I am sorry to say one of my side, in my opinion very rudely, said it was a fake. Dunsany said, 'What do you mean by fake?' The answer was 'Well! You could not show the name on my arm.' Dunsany said, 'I am not so sure about that, I will try.' So the performance was gone through again, but when the gentleman bared his arm and had the ash rubbed all over it, no name appeared. 'There! I told you so,' was remarked. 'Yes!' says Dunsany, 'but your arm is all black.' I think he had the laugh, and I for one was delighted at the young man's discomfiture.

On another occasion, Lord Dunsany, knowing he was sure to be asked to do some tricks, while dressing for dinner, asked the butler in the house where he was staying, if he could cash a cheque with a £5 note; the butler found one, but was told that it did not matter after all. After dinner, when asked to do a trick, he asked if anyone had a £5 note. Fortunately, no-one had, so they rang the bell and the servant produced one, and Dunsany then said he would endeavour to tell the number; he put a wet towel round his head and remained with his head between his knees for some five minutes, during which time there was to be absolute silence and everyone was to will him to read the number. Of course, if there were any unbelievers it made it much more difficult. Eventually, much exhausted and with great effort, he put down the number of the note on a piece of paper and it marvellously proved to be correct.

(1932)

It's the first time he's played for us so I don't know how fast he is, but he's certainly got the build for it.'

(1976)

CRUSOE'S ISLAND
The World of R. C. Robertson-Glasgow

TALKING AT RANDOM

The complete captain in cricket is as rare as the Dodo. You get skilful tacticians who are quite unaware of the infinite variety of individual temperaments; and you get consummate handlers of men who know no more about tactics than a water-buffalo. You get military-minded captains who treat the cricket field as a parade-ground; and you get absent-minded romantics who let things take what course they will, and have their fast bowler standing permanently at long-leg.

Even the experts disagree on what constitutes top-grade captaincy, just as modern informed opinion has come round to the view that Wellington was in many respects a greater leader than Napoleon. My own favourite captain was a boy of twelve in school cricket. Equable and unobservant, he kept wicket with memorable incompetence, and, when struck on the back of the head by a slick return from his long-stop, he said, 'I wish you wouldn't do that.' If self-restraint be a sign of good captaincy, that wicket-keeper must rate very high indeed.

Douglas and Daniell
In the more exalted and senior realms of the game, I had much admiration for J.W.H.T. Douglas, of Essex and England. He captained England against Australia in high triumph and resounding defeat. At his best, he was a great opening bowler, of fast-medium pace. Above all, he was a fighter. He loved the battle, and never gave in. Little, less than little, did he care if critics or crowds disapproved of his policies.

I had the luck to play under him once, and to stay as a guest in his London flat, where Mrs J.W.H.T. ruled with firm kindness. One evening, I absent-mindedly left the bath-tap running too long, and returned to find the place under water. A frantic and furious lady who lived below had to be calmed and we apologised. As she receded, Johnny Douglas said to me, with a grin, 'I *thought* that the flood would make her come up for a talk.'

He had the gifts that are needed to become Amateur Middleweight Boxing Champion of the World, winning a hairline decision in the Olympic Games over an Australian, 'Snowy' Baker. Tough he was, with shining black hair and tremendous forearms. An Essex player once told me how a very fast bouncer hit Douglas's head on its way to the boundary. Fielders approached him with expressions of concern; but Johnny waved them away with 'What's the matter? It counts four, doesn't it?' and so, in those days, it deservedly did.

But, for those who knew, he wasn't just tough and determined. He was an expert ballroom dancer; and he tried, in vain, to conceal a heart of pure gold. Once, when on a soccer tour (another accomplishment), Douglas went to a sort of dance-cum-cabaret in Paris. Very soon it was evident that the alleged star of the cabaret had lost her shine. She was 'getting the bird'. Douglas, seeing her distress, got up from his table and made her join him in an impromptu dancing sequence which brought the house down.

Maybe Johnny Douglas was not a very astute tactician. But as a leader, as an inspiration to the pessimistic or faint-hearted, he had few equals.

My own captain, most of the time, in Somerset, was John Daniell. He had also captained England at rugger. He, too, was a magnificent, and not taciturn, leader. Indeed, he had an unrivalled gift of various and frequently deserved invective. He had much to try him. Jim Bridges and I, who sometimes opened the bowling, also fancied ourselves as batsmen. Once, we said to our captain. 'John, what have these opening batsmen of ours got that we haven't?' 'An average of over ten,' said Daniell. On another occasion I asked him where he wanted me to bat, and he said: 'If I had my way, you wouldn't bat at all.' A great personality; a great silly-point; a batsman ever at his best when others weren't; a captain under whom it was delightful and instructive to play.

Chapman and Jardine
Then, there were two captains who led England to victory in Australia by four Test matches to one. Cricket made us friends: A. P. F. Chapman and D. R. Jardine; wholly different in character, but each, without question, great in his kind. Percy Chapman was the Prince Rupert of the game; gay, debonair, dashing, but astutely observant; in his prime, one of the most dangerous left-handed batsmen of this century, and a fielder of unbelievable brilliance. He had the flair and the crowd-appeal.

109

Douglas Jardine I knew from schooldays onwards. Part of his character was sheer Cromwell; the other part was all wit and kindness. It is as an Ironside that most fellow-players and opponents will remember him. In modern parlance, no-one, not even the incredible Bradman, was going to make a Charlie of Jardine. So, there raged for some months in Australia during 1932–33, the Great Bodyline Battle. Long ago the dust has settled. In more recent years, visiting Australian cricketers found the hospitality and humour of him who was once their Enemy No. 1.

To each of these captains and friends I would like to say goodbye. We are left with memories untold.

> 'For, Death he taketh all away,
> But them he cannot take.'

OXFORD MEMORIES

Let us leave Lord's a moment, the crown of the University season, and go to Oxford itself. Go by that best of railways, which the great Brunel conceived over a hundred years ago, or, if you love your Thames, by road through Henley, along the winding river with its thick-clustered trees, through Saxon Dorchester, and into the noblest of all main streets, the Oxford High, with Magdalen as its sentinel. Then, if you want a very redundance of beauty, turn northwards to the Parks; loveliest almost of cricket grounds, with its famous tree under which the patient and determined few wait for the showers to stop, where there gathers year by year, to watch and talk and unravel the inexhaustible past, the noble band of devoted perennials, faithful men who still tell you, as if it were but yesterday, of Tip Foster and Charles Fry, and of years long before that; where the white-tied candidate, escaped at last from Logic's accursed bonds, may be seen breathing with joy the purer air, dispersing Aristotle and Bishop Stubbs and Ancient Manorial Rights with the sight of green grass and the click of the ball in the wicket-keeper's gloves; where there stalks majestic from the croquet ground that eminent geographer, displaying to best advantage his well-tried mallet, as who should say, 'Ah, yes, young fellow, don't talk to me of cricket: here is a game for those of riper years, a game of pure skill and, I may say, of unalloyed technique.'

The Parks, where the blissful perambulator is pushed along by the nurse ignorant of the howitzer that some Bettington or Hewetson has this moment sent hissing over their innocent heads; the Parks through which, in the longer and wetter grass, Tom Hayward used to search with vain mutterings for the ball which he had bowled from a distance of sixteen yards, and had seen pulled relentlessly and with abandoned joy from outside the off-stump to deep mid-wicket. The shadow of change comes over this Elysian playing-field but little. Sometimes, when a new season starts, a well-known face is not to be seen, a once familiar cry of 'Oh, well played, sir!' merges into an echo from the fading past. But cricket at Oxford is a conservative old party, and likes to keep his friends about him. They may not be many, but they are devoted.

Mellow vintage and foaming beer

Exchange for this mellow vintage, this Caecuban from the ancestral cellar, a good old English beer, and come to the Oval, where, as you stand outside the dressing-room on fine days, the Houses of Parliament 'like a mist rise into towers', and below there stretches out the marvellous turf, where Hobbs has, on Saturdays, made happier so many crowds already disposed to be happy; where Jessop played his immortal innings; where Sam Woods fizzed the ball over Bobby Abel's head and then strode out of the Pavilion, chin first, to sustain the sliding fortunes of Somerset; where Hewetson, not unmindful of his great original, hit a Surrey bowler, in 1923, three times on end against the bricks of the pavilion. The Oval is of a more rough-hewn essence than Lord's. It is the difference between bludgeon and rapier. You can go to the Oval in a cloth cap and get away with it, unless you throw it in the air and some neighbour puts it on for his own. How many hearts (and twice as many feet) have been broken on that perfect wicket! It is there that, at last, the bowlers 'cease because they are few'; there that they give you so good a lunch that you forget your weary limbs; there that you begin to rejoice when three of Surrey are out for 200, only to turn your joy to weeping when Jardine succeeds Shepherd, and, if that classic willow for once is unfruitful, Fender and Peach send you to far corners of the vast oasis; there that you make the acquaintance of spectators who have paid their shilling to see you run; there that, as you retrieve the breathless seven, you view the gasometer from a novel angle; there, lastly, that you wonder why on earth your captain is such a deluded idiot as to lose the toss on a cloudless Saturday! It is real English beer at the Oval, and if at times it foams over a little who minds? What if, at Oxford, the spectators are too polite to ask you to bend in the field? We know their thoughts, though unexpressed? What if they never seem to care who wins at the Parks?

We know they do, and they care quite as much as the crowd at the Oval; only the method of demonstration differs. I often think that, while the spirit of the noble peers who played with his Grace the Duke of Marlborough pervade Marylebone and its soft green trees, at the Oval there survives something of the cheerful lusty Saxons whom they lured to field for them on those summer evenings years ago. I have always loved the Oval, however many runs have flowed from the opposing bats. For there, one day, Tom Raikes and I misunderstood one another. We were batting for Oxford against Surrey. It is useless to ask me what happened, for I shall never know: this much is certain; we had completed a run, and then the fun started – Yes – No – No – Yes – Go back – All right then, don't. Twice we were running abreast to the same end; we each had won one race, and were about to begin the final when Strudwick unkindly put the other wicket down. Where was the ball meanwhile? Ah, where indeed? I had made some 25, so elected to stay in, and Raikes went away, cheerfully calling out, 'It was all my fault,' which it wasn't. The laughter

"LONDON'S OWN."

(1921)

at length died down, and I was preparing for the next ball, when Hitch, at short leg, murmured in a hoarse voice, 'You know who was out really?' He didn't know at all; nor did the umpires, and now no-one ever will know.

Brighton's champagne

Don't think now of the Varsity match. It is only a faint sub-conscious menace. You have sipped your old wine at Oxford, drained off your frothing beer at Kennington; now for the champagne of Brighton. Brighton with its clanging trams which sway along towards Lewes and the Dyke, with its intriguing cosmopolity, its Aquarium, now alas defunct, its glorious air blowing from the white-crested sea: Brighton with its eager hordes of schoolboys and schoolgirls, foretaste of a greater invasion at Eastbourne, armed with pencils that will not write, and smiles that constrain the malingerer, nevertheless, to try. Brighton with its white cliffs rolling away to Rottingdean and Telscombe. The home of so many of Kipling's fairy imaginings. There we used to meet the ever-youthful, ever-hospitable, Harry Preston, with his pictures of old boxers, stars in the firmament in the days when Sir Charles Tregellis drove his phaeton from London at fifteen rollicking miles an hour: drink in the infinite variety of his conversation; yes, and his Napoleon brandy as well. There we talked finance and politics with George Robey, something rather less exacting with George Graves. There, in the lounge, our tame reporter, Philip Browne, played his Beethoven Sonatas. There, one famous year, in the Albion, stayed the Executive Council of the Labour Party.

Breathes there a man with soul so dead, who, as he plays against Sussex at Brighton and bowls on that perfect wicket, has not thought of the palmy days of English batting, when Ranji's silk shirt fluttered in the breeze, and the bowler watched with a wondering dismay as his best and fastest sped, with a wizard glance, to the leg-boundary; when Charles Fry's broad bat and iron back-play were waiting for you at the other end. They couldn't always get the other side out, I know; that would have ruined the Championship. They had no Tate then, bowling opening overs fit to make the gods weep tears of amber, to win the matches after those great ones had made defeat well-nigh impossible.

But we must away. Back again to Lord's, to play the MCC. No vintage is this; something more medicinal perhaps. This is our dress-rehearsal; it seldom went well, and always set the critics buzzing. The chinks in the armour, under their searching pens, became, so often, gaping wounds. But it was good for the soul; for in everything, games as well, London is not slow to find a true standard of performance. Our arms were not high enough, or perhaps too high, we played back more than the great ones had been accustomed to do, our fielding was not the fielding of young men; there was an insouciance, a lethargy almost in our very demeanour. So we were told; and so we never believed, at least not much of it! But how salutary these criticisms were! For nothing is more nauseous than the accounts of matches which burgeon with superlatives, where the ordinary grows into the excellent, and the good parades as the wholly magnificent. I cannot say that I ever loved these games, necessary and instructive as they were. I would have preferred to have seen that turf for the first time in the year only on the day of days. To me it seemed like an inverted anti-climax, like walking a battlefield before instead of after the great struggle. Two memories, however, stand out like towers above that rather uninteresting waste. A century by G. N. Foster, who played like an angel, when others were failing; and a great match-winning innings by Hendren, when the club was set a vast score to make.

Archbishop of the Dining Room

And then Eastbourne. For Oxford the epilogue of the tour. The liqueur brandy in which we drowned for the wonderful present all thoughts of the future. And yet, though nothing could surpass the social delights of that match, there linked a haunting little demon in the cricket. A place, perhaps, was still to be filled, and what 'Varsity player can pretend that he knows no difference between playing with and playing for his Blue? Even

that little memento-mori, however, and it popped up but seldom, failed to disturb the epicurean pleasure of the whole festival. Utterly different from Brighton, Eastbourne preserves its own particular, perennial charm. Brighton always seems to be preparing for Saturday, Eastbourne to be recovering from Sunday. Brighton is diffuse, Eastbourne concentrated, and for us it was concentrated in the Grand Hotel, with its huge lounge, buzzing with talk and music, in 'Shrimp' Leveson-Gower and the Mayor of Eastbourne, and their annual passages of wit in the marquee speeches, in sounds of revelry by night, in desperate games of snooker, in Mr Gabb, Archbishop of the Dining Room, in moonlight drives to Beachy Head, in dancing to 'Jenky's' band, in never-ending gaieties. As to cricket, the scoring was generally high, and the batting distinctly diverting. I remember Bettington making 100 in two consecutive years. He nearly cracked the cylinder of a motor-bicycle, and soon after, from the sea end, hit a screamer which rootled the birds' nests and finally landed near an old gentleman who was in the act of performing a 'roquet' on the lawn beyond. Those three days used to pass like the wind, then came the weekend of recuperation; for me, when possible, the hills of Hindhead, where I once, as a small boy, used to dream of bowling an invincible batsman with an irresistible googly . . . Past Willington and Polegate we drive, reflecting on recent enormities, or thinking, with a tinge of regret, that we will never play at Eastbourne again except as hoary graduates.
(1928)

OUR WICKET-KEEPER

It is not absolutely certain who asked Pogson to keep wicket; but it was a good idea, because he has an artificial leg which clicks and is worth an appeal almost any time with a strange umpire and, of course, this click works both ways, and sometimes a real catch is foisted on to his leg; and that leads to any amount of discussion.

He stands a long way back to the mediums, and so suffered much interference from Bellows, the slip fielder, who likes to peck in on the easier catches, on the understanding that they wouldn't carry to the wicket-keeper. But he got Bellows moved to long-leg, and now there is no slip at all.

Nor could he come to any working agreement with Piers about his googly. At first, they arranged that every time Piers meant to bowl his googly, he should say 'up a bit, point'; but point said he was far too close already, so this plan fell through. Then it was settled that Piers should announce the googly with an obvious scowl, but, as he was nearly always in a rage with the umpire over lbws, nothing came of that. Next, they agreed that, before the googly, Piers should shout 'oi.' But a visiting batsman objected, and so that matter rests where it began.

Pogson brought off a catch in July, and this has made him rather interfering. Last Saturday, when the score was 148 for 3 and the captain said 'Have a try this end, Major,' Pogson said, 'No.' He was overruled, but, when the first ball was returned from the square-leg boundary, he examined it all round, whistled, then rolled it back all along the ground; 'to test the bias,' he said. 'In the air, please,' remarked the Major. 'Not for you,' replied Pogson.

He is keenly sensitive to any irregularities in the surface of the pitch, and, having pointed them out to the bowler, he will shout 'up a bit' or 'two points west' after the delivery. This habit is sometimes resented by opponents. An argument on this head arose a fortnight back with a bald-headed batsman, which ended only when Pogson said, 'and put your cap on. You remind me of the Oval.'

Sometimes he wears a green blazer with thin mauve stripes; 'The Wanderers,' he says. 'We used to have a tour in August. In those days I was a fast bowler.' But, except the blazer, no record of this itinerant team seems to remain. He bats now at number eleven, and keeps his pads on throughout the match. '*Semper paratus*,' he says.

(1942)

Notable among fine bats is the Wisden DENIS COMPTON, with which this famous player achieved his great batting feats last year. Among Wisden cricket balls, a favourite is the *Lords Special*, as used on the 1948-9 South African Tour. Another well-known ball is *Duke's Special County*, which is also used in Test Matches and by the County and leading Clubs.

WISDEN CRICKET EQUIPMENT
STOCKED BY LEADING SPORTS OUTFITTERS

(1949)

OUR UMPIRE

DRAG
By Bernard Hollowood

I had as good a view as anybody. I was fielding at mid-on. Springall came up to bowl from about 12 yards, planked his right foot down a good three inches behind the bowling crease and let fly. The two yells 'Huzzatt!' and 'N'ball!' were simultaneous. The Chedsley opening batsman (he was wearing a Polytechnic cap) rubbed his upper thigh as a cloud of Blanco mushroomed from his left pad just above the ankle and gradually dispersed.

Springall returned to his bowling mark deep in thought. We waited for him to make the silly scuffing *chassé* that launches him into his run. But he stood still, like a man waiting for a 6A bus.

'D'you mind standing back?' he said politely to the umpire.

The umpire backed a couple of paces.

'A bit farther,' said Springall.

'You're dragging,' said the umpire. 'I shall no-ball you even if I stand by the sight-screen.' (Actually, we have no screens at Whiteheath, and we all thought it pretty bad form for a visiting umpire to draw attention to the fact.)

'Never been no-balled in all my 20 years,' said Springall. And he was about to say more when he became aware that his captain, from first slip, was signalling to him to carry on. He charged up to the wicket.

'N'ball!' screamed the umpire, and the ball went for four, just missing mid-on's left shoulder.

'What's that for then?' said Springall.

'Dragging.'

'Dragging my foot!' said Springall redundantly. 'I'm bowling as I've always bowled.'

'I've no doubt,' said the umpire, 'but this is 1960. Now I'll be reasonable. You put your back foot down three feet behind the crease and I'll pass you. Otherwise, you've had it. I'm sorry, but the law's the law.' Then from his coat pocket he drew a white circular object which turned out, surprisingly, to be a Continental beer mat and placed it carefully one long stride back from the crease.

Springall completed the over with two long-hops and two full tosses, with one of which he hit the Chedsley opener loud and clear in the pit of the stomach. The over cost 16 runs.

During Harris's over Springall and the captain were in consultation.

'Let me change ends, Skip.'

'Well, all right, but Harris won't like it. You know as well as I do he always prefers that end, where he's got his arm in the cedars and the chance of pitching on the ridge.' (This ridge is a feature of the Whiteheath wicket: it is a minor earthwork dating from the last war and certain Home Guard manoeuvres with a Churchill tank over a terrain the consistency of hot jam.)

'He won't no-ball Harris,' said Springall.

'Care to bet? If he's as keen as this on dragging he's probably on the lookout for bent arms and all that. Still, might as well try it. They're 20 already and I reckon 50's a winning total today. I'll throw an over up myself, and you can take the next one at Harris's end.'

Harris was baffled by the change, but he is a good team man and accepted the move merely as additional support for his view that City stockbrokers make helpless captains of village clubs.

The skipper's over increased the Chedsley score to 32. Then Harris bowled. His first two balls were uneventful except that the batsman put up a dolly to point off the first, and broke his bat hitting a six off the second. The third ball was a very short long hop. Slow-medium.

'I'm warning you,' said the umpire. 'Any more bumpers this over and I shall report you.'

'Who to?' said Harris, in genuine perplexity.

'Never you mind who!' said the umpire . . .

Thirty-five for no wicket.

The trouble started when the visiting umpire saw that Springall was about to bowl from the other, the home, end. Immediately he walked across – Chester-like – to consult *our* umpire. There was much gesticulation, the opposing captain ran out from the pavilion, the deep-fielders lay down, the batsmen sat on their bats. Carless at third man lit a cigarette.

Our captain stuck to his guns and refused to allow the visiting umpire to change ends in pursuit of Springall. The visiting captain apologised and urged his man to go easy with his conscience and interpretation of the laws. The umpires quarrelled, waved their arms about, and there, suddenly, was the Chedsley man's pipe flying from his mouth. He picked it up and left the field. Our man followed. Springall, almost in tears, ran to his motorbike and roared away without paying his tea-money.

The game was resumed, without umpires, and ended in a tie, 57-all.

I have the beer mat as a souvenir.

Published by courtesy of PUNCH.

(1960)

SNEEZED OUT, OR HOW AN UMPIRE WAS AVENGED
By Henry Grierson

By and large you will agree the finest appealers are fast bowlers and wicket-keepers. The latter, as we all know, leap a yard in the air with ball in hand and fairly let it go; the fast bowler rotates as he yells, thus facing the umpire with hands aloft, or with hands on knees in a menacing position, which is also much favoured.

But I bet none of you has had the unique honour of hearing a batsman sneezed out, as I have, and off his own bowling. That makes you pull up your little cotton socks or tights.

I was bowling for Leicester Ivanhoe, and the batsman and square-leg umpire were son and father respectively. Thrice had our wicket-keeper appealed for stumping, and each time had been turned down by the batsman's father, as was his habit, as it was said. Meantime our umpire, I observed, had adopted a somewhat stern mien, if you follow me.

The very next over, I bowled one at least a foot outside the off-stump, which that batsman played with his pad. At the same moment Gordon Salmon, that great pillar of Ivanhoe cricket over the years, who stood at mid-off, let out a truly magnificent sneeze, whereupon our umpire raised his fore-finger and roared 'OUT.'

As the batsman walked slowly from the scene I looked at our umpire and raised the old bushy eyebrows. Getting the message he licked his lips in satisfaction, jerked his thumb in the direction of his counterpart and remarked with utmost relish, 'I done it because of that there.'

The late George H. Wharmby (Lancs, Notts and Beds) used his great stature, lordly looks and an appeal in a note of such high pitch that would have put to shame many a prima donna, and often brought excellent results in otherwise doubtful cases. And he had another admirable ploy when a batsman hit him over his head, which he deeply resented. At long-off stood the late Bert Holdstock, remembered with affection at

Five Ways of Asking "OWAZAT"?

THE ART OF THE APPEAL

Reproduced by kind permission of 'Punch.'
(1960)

Luton. As the batsmen were about to complete the first run and watching the crease, George, with split-second timing, would roar, 'Let 'er come, Bert,' when Holdstock, in point of fact, was still yards away from the ball. But the magic nearly always worked – 'No, get back,' the apprehensive batsman would shout, then adding, somewhat shamefacedly, 'Sorry, we might have done.'

Only once, during a long association, did I see George Wharmby utterly defeated on an appeal; this was during a Beds v Suffolk match, the batsman involved being Walter Quaife, elder brother of the famous W. G. Quaife, the Warwicks and England stylist. Walter drove George into the covers and called, but the ball was beautifully intercepted by the late Herbie Sutherland, a splendid all-round sportsman, who returned it to Wharmby with Quaife yards from home.

But in his excitement George had accidentally removed the bails with his elbow, thus I shouted 'Pull up a stump.' He gathered all three in his enormous right hand, flung them on the deck and rent the heavens with an appeal. 'Not out,' said Rudd, the excellent umpire, and George nearly fainted. But Rudd was right, although the Law was not so clear as it is today, when Law 31 states that if both bails be off the bowler may pull up a stump, 'provided that the ball is held in the hand or hands so used.'

You budding Fiery Freds have been warned.

(1969)

THE LADY UMPIRE
By Lady Flora Poore

A July afternoon and ideal cricket weather. A great match was to be played between Puddleworth and Fiddleton. We drove to the scene of action, a large meadow with a neat square of mown grass and rolled pitch, surrounded by a ball-resisting outfield. Little did I dream of the part in the struggle I – a poor female – was to play!

Having settled myself comfortably in the car to watch from a safe distance, I heard a murmuring inquiry among the cricket stalwarts as to who was umpiring. There was one umpire deficient. A consultation followed, after which, my husband – who was playing for Puddleworth – made for my car. 'Will you umpire?' he said. Now although not entirely ignorant in the laws of cricket, having been born in the atmosphere of a cricketing father and keeping on the tradition by marrying a first-class cricketer, it was a giddy height above mere watching knowledge to umpire at a match – albeit but a village one. But as 'fools step in where wise men fear to tread', I consented to fill the breach.

I knew that appeals in village cricket were frequent and in my mind uprose past visions of matches I had watched and umpires' decisions disputed hotly as the warrior returned to the pavilion. 'Never touched it!' 'Hit me shoulder!' 'I was more'n a yard in.' '*He's* no umpire!' and suchlike. The possibility of nasty chances needed eyes and ears 'skinned' so to speak, if I was to answer correctly without a shade of hesitation the dreaded 'How's that?' The bowler's footwork, the pitch of the ball for lbw, the catch at the wicket if from on, or below the wrist, the wide, and so on – such a list! Could I possibly get through it! Then the automatic transference of pennies from hand to pocket for the overs.

Having survived my first over I removed to the other point of vantage at sqare leg, which entailed a fresh vista of decisions in runu outs, stumping, etcetera, and my concentration eliminated the watch for such trifles as doubtful bowling action from the far wicket! At the back of my cowardly feminine mind, too, was the lurking fear of a ball at my head. But my greatest dread was his innings and I knew it had to come.

I saw him stalking down to the pitch, bat under arm, pulling on his gloves. Was I to be the factor to dismiss him! Horrible thought! For the first time in my life I almost hoped he would come out quickly in an undoubted obvious way – to the other umpire's decision. Added to which he would be able then to relieve me as umpire.

I gave him 'leg stump' and then stood concentrated, palpitating, and praying that no appeals might be lodged. The six coins were transferred from hand to pocket. Survival so far and the next over a slight slackening of tension as from the leg point of view I had no fears. But once again behind the wicket and chances arising in my brain like ghouls. Runs came pleasantly and many overs passed. Then the inevitable! In playing at a low off ball he hit the ground hard – the ball sped on into the wicket-keeper's hands – but not from his bat, though the closeness and noise brought the dreaded 'How's that?' 'Not out!' came from a weak female voice – weak from fright but decisive in tone. I looked sideways for dissentient voices or angry eyes. All seemed satisfied. A grateful thrill passed down my back.

The match ended soon after that in a victory for Puddleworth. I had given eight decisions, all of which, barring the last seemed to have met with approval, and in this last my judgment was contested; but the batsman was so bulky that his body entirely obliterated the wickets. How could I tell if they would have been hit or not! Though it didn't signify as he came out – obviously – next ball!

I returned to the car, exhausted mentally and bodily.

(Annual, 1932–33)

DO UMPIRES HIBERNATE?
By M.H. Stevenson

Where do umpires go in the winter time? Do they hibernate? Do they inhabit some murky limbo set apart from the rest of humanity? Or do they relinquish the robes of their judicial deity and mingle freely in the everyday world?

Those who have read my revolutionary new cricket publication entitled *Incontrovertible Proof, after Vast Research, that the Umpire is Definitely Human* (Zizzbaum and Flukestein, 45s), will be familiar with the two main psychological types to which an umpire may belong, and will have guessed the answer to these questions.

Firstly – the *'Outer'* – large of frame, rubicund of countenance, who drinks pints and eats vastly, is a gay, carefree fellow, who, in his playing days, was a fast bowler and who now has only to hear somebody in the crowd clear his throat for his finger to shoot aloft. This type, often suffering from arthritis or severe spraining of the wrist through over-exercise, might lessen the chances of chronic injury by standing with the business finger permanently pointing skyward and draped with a cloth bearing a skull and crossbones.

The *'Outer'* is best exemplified by a certain Irish umpire, who on one occasion was so imbued with partisan fervour, that when his team's star bowler struck the batsman on the leg some eighteen inches outside the off-stump, he was the only person on the field to shout for lbw – and fair-minded enough to turn down the appeal.

On another occasion a celebrated *'Outer'*, whose son, keeping wicket, had appealed to him at square-leg following an impressively neat piece of stumping, was heard to mutter, 'Bloody marvellous, Son.' The *'Outer'* is not hard to spot!

Similarly, the *'Not-Outer'* bears his own unmistakable marks of identification. He is very small,

"*Crikey!*"

That's Shell— *—that was!"*

YOU CAN BE SURE OF SHELL

(Spring Annual, 1938)

(1960)

wizened, misanthropic, drinks half shandies and eats sparingly. During his playing days he escaped from the unwelcome criticism of a nagging wife by opening the innings (strokelessly) for the local Works XI and suffered regular and consistently unjust dismissals at the hands of his future colleague, the extrovert '*Outer*'.

Covered, as he has been almost from birth, by sweaters and criticism, it is not suprising that the poor '*Not-Outer*' takes a jaundiced view of life in general and bowlers in particular. To him the batsman appears as the bridge-defending Horatius or the vicarious sufferer for his own life of insult and affront.

He is best typified by the perennial story of the village umpire standing during a charity match while a famous fast bowler operated against the local opener who was dismissed, caught twice and lbw, by the first three deliveries which he received. The local '*Not-Outer*', easily master of the situation, refused to allow the batsman to depart, whereupon the now enraged gladiator projected the fourth ball of the over with such velocity that it broke the middle stump, and turning to the umpire said, 'Nearly got him that time.'

One '*Not-Outer*' is supposed to have refused a legitimate appeal for lbw in an evening Cup match, on the grounds that the ball was keeping too low!

And now to answer the question – 'Where *do* umpires go in the winter time?' Whether the '*Outers*' are butchers, salesmen, auctioneers, farmers or 'tick-tack' men; or the '*Not-Outers*' Customs officials, Inland Revenue officers, private detectives or shop stewards they remain with us. And as soon as we reach for linseed oil or embrocation in April they will gather like vultures around the cricket grounds of the world, mentally practising with our first net their own penchant for delirious dismissal or stern denial.

(1963)

GARDENING COLUMN

THE NEW DRAINS AT LORD'S WILL RUIN
THE MUSHROOMS
By John Reason

Archaeologically, the dig at Lord's to put in the new drains has been a terrible disappointment. Surely there should have been something interesting underneath all that hallowed turf. A few old coins, perhaps. The site of a Roman encampment. The shell of an ancient sailing barge. An illuminated scroll, even, saying that Thomas Lord was here. But no. Nothing like that. Just a foot of soil, compacted like brick, some old fireclay drains, broken and clogged with silt, and three fairy rings.

I never would have noticed the fairy rings if it had not been for Jim, the Irish foreman in charge of the drain-laying. They are just off the square, at the Nursery end. Three dark olive circles in the grass. One of Jim's trenches slices right through them. I asked if that would not break the magic spell.

'Sure, and I wouldn't know about that,' says Jim. 'But if it was a nice soft, wet sort of day, I think maybe you could pick mushrooms off of them at five o'clock in the morning.'

Mushrooms at Lord's! Fairy rings! It's the wrong image entirely.

'Well,' says Jim defensively. 'They put different soils on as a top dressing, and maybe the mushroom spore got onto the grass then.'

He was quite sure about it.

Pavilion pond

Mr S.C. Griffith, MCC secretary, does not know about the mushrooms, but he does admit that he is disappointed about the archaeological void.

'I had hoped that we might find something,' he said. 'So much has happened on this ground. We even had a pond here once. A natural pond. It was in front of the pavilion. One of the early groundsmen learned to swim in it.'

But all the diggers found when they herring-boned the ground with their 2ft 6in trenches was a foot of soil which had been rolled so hard down the years that it was like rock. MCC have kept a piece of it in the office. It is shaped like a lump of coal, and it is about as hard.

'That was the cause of our trouble,' said Mr Griffith. 'For years and years, the outfield was rolled, without ever being spiked, and the water simply could not get through to the drains underneath. We did have drains there, and despite what the newspapers said, we have a perfectly good plan of them. But the water could not penetrate to them. The drains were put in about 60 years ago. So they would have come to the end of their useful life anyhow. That was why we decided, early in the summer, to put in the new system.'

The drainage was so bad that in a heavy storm, the water just slid down the eight foot slope to the Tavern in a surface sheet. It was this waterslide which caused the ridge on the wicket, or rather, as Mr Griffith reveals, the two ridges.

'There is one at each end,' he says, 'just short of what would be a length for the very quickest of bowlers. As the rainwater slid down the slope from the stand, it wore two channels across the square, each about an inch deep. If you went on the ground in a heavy storm, you could see them quite clearly. In one place the pitch was under water. In another you could see the blades of grass. We put top dressing on to build up the level, but in really heavy rain most of that gets washed away.'

Work began in September and it should be completed in a few days' time. This will leave plenty of time for the ground to recover for next season.

The herringbone pattern of the drains points down the hill to the Tavern. Fireclay pipes, about three inches in diameter and about fifteen inches long, are laid end to end, without being joined, in the bottom of each trench. Then clinker is packed on top and graduated soil backfilled to the turf.

The grass is very shallow-rooted. It had to be. The poor stuff hadn't a hope of penetrating the cake of soil. This was what made spiking such a frightening operation on the occasions when it was tried at Lord's.

'We knew we should do it,' said Mr Griffith, 'but as each tine went in, it tore up a huge clod of earth. I got the wind up, and we stopped it. But the people at Bingley say we must spike the whole ground, and that we must do it twice a week.'

The fairies won't like it, and it will ruin the mushrooms.

(1964)

(1921)

WHAT IS 'A TERRIBLY GOOD SHOT'?
By 'Bomber' Wells

My pint and I were pinned into a corner of 'the local' the other evening and required to define the expression 'a *terribly* good shot'. I was *frightfully* nonplussed and said thanks *most awfully* when my inquisitor agreed to let me have notice of that question. Pondering it as I looked in at the next Saturday's game I noted that John Hampshire had one attributed to him and concluded that it could mean a good counter played to a bad ball or a bad one played to a good ball, but that in either cases the *terribly* was *most awfully* redundant. So in most instances was any comment at all. Just gratuitous pieces of non-information prefixed by a sawn-off superlative signifying nothing and, like my glass sir, quite empty.

I'd like to go on a tour myself, a quick one round England, taking with me the readers who are not quite sure why the wickets vary so much and therefore the style of play too. Why an attack brilliantly successful in one county would flop in another.

Let's head first for the coast; to Essex, Surrey, Sussex, Kent and Hants, areas traditionally inclined to lean mostly on seam bowlers. Their wickets are usually green and firm; the ball, carefully polished on one side of the seam to abet its unpredictable progress, wobbles in the air and cuts off from the wicket in never-alike tangents. Your seam-up bowler, in the first hour or so, while the wicket remains firm (sometimes first *and* last), is the backbone of his side and can be deployed with telling effect. Since counties like these have to field a number of seam bowlers they also require that they be all-rounders, and produce some brilliant ones into the bargain.

Up the M1 now to the Midlands and the North, taking in Worcester, Warwicks, Leics, Northants, Notts, Derby, Lancs and Yorks. Given the right weather and care, the wickets presented by these counties make first-class batting wickets, different climatic-atmospheric conditions holding sway. So nearly all the sides in these counties offer more varied attacks; speed, medium-pace and spin. Some of the greatest batsmen England has known were bred in these areas, and scores of the real fast men as well. Bowlers like Larwood, Voce, Trueman, Statham, Tyson, to name a few.

For a model wicket, a consistent 'good 'un', we must go to Lord's, that place capable of striking terror into the stoutest of cricketing hearts. Many great feats have been performed here, and many great feet belonging to clottish performers would have been better kept off its turf. Once upon a time the wicket at Lord's was guarded by the infamous 'ridge' which on occasions gave rise to suggestion that the bowler was using a tennis ball, so odd was the bouncing around that went on. Now, with the eyes of the television world coldly scrutinising each blade of grass, the wickets are usually above reproach. Not that this latest Test wicket was exactly a paragon.

Over the river at the Oval, or the 'Burma Road', as it was commonly called in the Fifties, a batting wicket of impeccable trim is without fail presented, though again this was not always the case in the past. Finally across to 'God's Country' and mine, the glorious West, where spin bowlers hang around the pavilion just waiting a chance to bowl, where off-breaks can become 'leggers' by the seam pitching the right way, no thanks to the finesse of the bowler. At Taunton a wicket can be produced as good and better than most in the country. In Glamorgan the wickets are *rather* prone to 'do a bit', as the television gentlemen would say. Similar to the Gloucester ones; slow, low and be blowed. These counties have provided some great spinners, who are the most economical on these wickets.

Whatever the county, we are entitled to expect good wickets, with only the elements to blame for disconcerting variations. On the county ground, that is. But for cricket to survive the counties have had to take the game to the people, to local pitches. These grounds may be picturesque, but they mostly fail to present wickets that can stand the rigours of a three-day match. Which remark eases me into position for a closing thump on my old drum. Now you see why your county cricket professional has claimed to be the world of sport's most versatile performer: day in and day out of slogging away under conditions never the same long enough for him to get the hang of them in time to fool you he's working hard when he ain't.

(1969)

SOME CURIOUS WICKETS
By Historicus

It is open to doubt whether any County Championship match, or any other game of such importance, had ever been played on so curious a wicket as that on which Worcestershire and Somerset contended a few days ago. The Worcester ground had suffered severely from floods, and for some time it was questionable whether it would be possible for the game to take place there; a most welcome spell of fine weather, however, enabled the fixture to be retained, but the cricket took place on a pitch which, almost devoid of grass, had more the appearance of a road than of a wicket fit for a first-class county match.

Water had been over two feet deep in the Pavilion, and it was a fortunate thing for Worcestershire that they had not arranged for a series of matches there whilst the ground was flooded. The enclosure has been inundated several times, and punts have been used to reach the Pavilion. It has been said that, when the water has receded after a rising of the river, a deposit has been left which has proved beneficial to the ground; but that it is possible to have too much of such a good thing recent experience has shown. At no time can two inches of mud in the members' enclosure, or indisputable evidence of sheep-dip among various deposits, be welcome.

Another ground liable to floods has been that at Bath. When Hampshire went there in 1903 the water was three feet deep on part of the enclosure, and on the last day four feet, owing to the overflowing of the Avon. In the circumstances, it was not a little remarkable that the decision to abandon the match was not announced until the third day. On at least one other occasion the water has been squeezed from the pitch by light rollers so as to enable play to commence at as early a moment as possible. Strange though many occurrences have been at Bath, however, the good people there never made such a mistake as was once committed at Worcester, when the ground was, in error, sown with turnip seed instead of grass.

Probably not many people are aware that, for many years after the present Lord's ground was opened, there were two ponds on it. In one of them the well-known 'Steevie' Slatter taught himself to swim; he tied one end of a rope to a tree and passed the other round his body, so that when tired or in difficulty he could haul himself out. The Oval, too, used to be flooded by the overflowing of the Effra, a small river which ran along one side of the ground, but this, as it happened, proved eventually a blessing in disguise, for when an underground tunnel was made for its reception the soil removed was used for the construction of the terraces which have proved such a boon to spectators. Since then the wickets have never been flooded unexpectedly; had they been, perhaps fire-engines might have been employed for pumping off the water, as has been done successfully in India.

Declining to play at Lord's

The wickets used, even in great matches, in the early days of the game, must have been so rough that, if similar ones were provided now, they would assuredly be marked as unfit for play. Marl and similar substances were things then unknown in the preparation of pitches, and no attempt was made to provide a smooth strip of ground for the use of the contending sides. Much in this respect is revealed by the old code of Laws, the first of which was: 'The pitching of the first wicket is to be determined by the cast of a piece of money.' Games in those far-distant times were not drawn through heavy scoring, and many a present-day bowler must sigh for the condition which then obtained. The pitches provided at the St Lawrence ground, Canterbury, seem always to have been among the best provided, but in other centres even in comparatively modern days, it was far different. Many veterans can still recall both Sussex and Surrey declining to play at Lord's owing to the roughness of the ground. 'Felix', of Kent, when batting there, used to pad even his elbow, and W.G. could remember creases at headquarters being cut in the turf, not painted. The famous Pilch, when travelling round the country, used to include among his cricket paraphernalia a scythe wherewith to cut the grass between the wickets, for, to use an expression employed by 'Bob' Fitzgerald, the pitches on many grounds 'partook very much of the Grampian Hills,' so that only a civil engineer could do justice to them. Our soldiers and sailors, too, have in their wanderings indulged in the game on wickets composed of all kinds of things – sand, solid rock, sail-cloth, etc. – but doubtless they enjoyed their recreation as keenly as if it had been under perfect conditions.

What may be called freak wickets have, of course, been many, such as those provided when games have been played on the Goodwin Sands, the deck of the *Great Eastern*, the top of Table Mountain, and on ice. But what must be considered as one of the most remarkable used in a match of any importance must surely have been the one on the very backbone of a ridge of downs when the Gentlemen of Devon once played the Gentlemen of Dorset. The ground sloped away so rapidly on either side that long-leg had an excellent view of the batsmen clearly cut against the sky, while cover-point was completely out of sight. One man who benefited from these conditions was the late Rev. J.F. Scobell, for he was credited with a hit which, with overthrows, brought him in thirty-seven runs!

Both at Lord's and The Oval – on the latter ground in a match against the Australians – the wickets have occasionally been pitched parallel to the Pavilion, instead of at right-angles to it; but such procedure, at least in games of importance, has been rare. When the mentioned instance at The Oval occurred it was so that playing on worn turf might be avoided. Many times, after a match has commenced, the wicket has been found to be too long or too short. Thus, when Mr C.I. Thornton's Eleven had lost a couple of wickets at Cambridge against the University in 1885, it was discovered that the pitch measured twenty-three and a half yards, instead of the regulation twenty-two, and accordingly the game was re-started. As to wickets having been doctored surreptitiously or damaged maliciously, a good deal could, if necessary, be written; but such subjects are outside the province of this article.

(1924)

CRICKET IN FAR-FLUNG PLACES

CRICKET – AND SMOG – IN CALIFORNIA
By H. Brearley

Having travelled approximately 6,000 miles from London to Los Angeles I found myself staying with a cricketer with a not inconsiderable reputation in England, whom I shall call Mr X. So it was that on a Sunday morning in August we climbed into an ancient Chevrolet and started purring along the amazing Californian Highways towards the north side of LA where Pasadena was due to test its cricketing strength against another local side. Mr X and I had been invited to play for Pasadena and we arrived at the ground at Griffith Park at 11.45 for a twelve o'clock start, having travelled a mere 55 miles in 65 minutes without exceeding the speed limit of 65 mph. The highways in this part of the world certainly are a masterpiece of engineering, especially where some half-dozen of them seem to merge at the same point. Then it is that they interweave at various heights on pillars of concrete, forming an astonishing and intricate pattern.

The ground was pleasantly placed with trees around it, a range of mountains in the distance, and horses carrying film-star looking females galloping along the nearby tracks. All the matches are played on one of two grounds and different sides take turns as the 'home' team. This was our privilege today so members of our team were busy pinning down matting on the pitch. By 12.45, Joey, our West Indian captain, announced that we had lost the toss, much to the disgust of a Chinese gentleman who had no desire to field in a temperature of ninety-five. He wasn't the only one. After two of the batting side had been persuaded to don umpires' coats, the match began with Joey bowling medium paced away swingers from one end and Hyram B. Stellenbosch (a local name!) bowling slightly faster from the other. Two quick wickets fell and after forty minutes play, with the score at 11 for 2, I was surprised to hear Joey announce that it was time for a 'water break'! We all trooped off for drinks from an ice box and as the temperature was now bordering on 100, the pause and the drinks were most welcome. These water breaks occurred periodically throughout the match and certainly could be looked on as an additional weapon for use by the fielding captain. In England we can only fall back on tea breaks or bonfires in adjacent allotments to provide distractions.

Smog trouble

Scoring was slow. There was no pace in the wicket but, more important, the grass in the outfield was so thick that the only way to hit a boundary was to lift the ball almost for a six. The most powerful cover drive on the ground produced only one run so that an individual score of 30 or so was quite extraordinary. But the most astonishing thing about the afternoon was the Smog. Most of us associate California with sunshine and beaches, film stars and bathing beauties but LA certainly has one more claim to fame. Apparently on some days, the mountains prevent the free movement of the air and fumes from innumerable motor cars remain suspended in the atmosphere reducing the visibility and making the mere process of breathing an unpleasant and difficult operation. How the fast bowlers managed to continue I don't know, and for the batsmen to run a three was to invite death by suffocation.

Tea was at 3.30. Tables were laid out under the trees laden with sandwiches, cakes, tea, and delicious pieces of melon and orange, and everyone gathered round informally. I found myself talking to our scorer, a lively gentleman 84 years old who recounted how he'd played his first game of cricket in the USA way back in 1921 and that he had been associated with the club ever since, playing his last match ten years ago. He had learnt his cricket in Bedfordshire.

We returned to fielding; the score crawled along; the temperature rose; the smog hurt one's chest. Would they never declare? Our bowlers were certainly too tired to get them out. Perhaps it was a mistake to play on the same side as a man with Mr X's reputation, although it was painfully obvious that the pitch and outfield would appreciably reduce his stature. After more than four hours' play our opponents declared with the enormous score of 156 for 8 and, as we were playing until 7.15 pm, or 7.30 if there was a chance of a result, we were left with a maximum batting time of 1 hour 50 minutes. One felt there was an element of caution in the declaration. Considering the conditions our

133

(1931–32)

fielding had stood up well to the task, only one person having had to leave the field because the heat and smog had made him feel sick. Our cover point, Frank, was particularly noticeable for the accuracy, speed and style of his throwing, not to mention his peaked cap. He was an ex-baseball player who had only recently taken up cricket and his returns would have done credit to Colin Bland!

Pull up de stumps

Joey's next problem was to persuade two members of his team to open the innings and after the long and tiring fielding session, any volunteer could have the job. Wickets fell quickly, including that of the captain of the United States Cricket XI – a man from Bolton, Lancashire! – and I went to the wicket with the score at twenty-five for three. I left at twenty-five for four, having driven a ball hard and low in the direction of mid-off only to see a tall black gentleman clap two enormous hands together, having moved them vertically in opposite directions, engulf the leather ball as though it were a peanut, and leap into the air with pleasure. So much for catching technique. Mr X proceeded to give a demonstration of the art of batting but eight wickets had fallen at the other end when Joey went into bat at ten past seven. By this time two of our side were umpiring and when at 7.14 an over was about to start, Joey edged up to one of the umpires and whispered through the side of his mouth in his West Indian drawl, 'If dey haven't claimed de extra time befoah 7.15 yo sure must pull up de stumps at de end of dis over!' So when the over came to an end, off walked Joey, up came the stumps, accompanied by frantic protestations from the opposition, who felt they were being robbed of victory. Long and heated arguments followed but Joey was adamant, and the final statement by the opposition captain – 'It's only a game and it doesn't matter who wins' – fell on incredulous ears after such a sporting declaration! Our final score was 76 for 8!

By the end of the match the sun had set, the smog had cleared, it was no longer unbearably hot and the mountains were at last revealed in all their beauty. After a few iced beers, the conditions of the afternoon and the quarrels of the evening were soon forgotten, and, as so often happens after cricket, friendships blossomed, colour and race were of no importance, and everyone departed happier for the day's exercise. In retrospect it was perhaps one of the most interesting games of cricket I have ever played in – although 12,000 miles is rather a long way to go to field for four hours and then get a duck!

(Spring Annual, 1968)

'BATTEN'
By R.G. Ingelse

As this book is written in Dutch we are unable to review it, but we think it will be of considerable interest to those who are interested in cricketana. It may be obtained from R. G. Ingelse at 102 Alkamadelaan, The Hague, Holland, at 1/6.

(1952)

SOME THOUGHTS
By C.B. Fry

One of the brilliant younger poets who was killed in the other Great War and who used to sign his verses in *The Westminster Gazette* with his nickname of 'Tip' (his full name was T.P. Cameron-Wilson) wrote a poignant little piece describing his feelings when home in England for a few days from the mud and murder of Flanders. A small poem much admired.

Suddenly in the midst of other and very different matter he paused and wrote:

'Kind God – and there's a cricket field.'

I perhaps misquote from memory but I do not obscure the point; the surprise of the line in that it seems quite appropriate to its alien setting.

A curious tribute to our game that the thought of it is not dissonant with the severities and miseries and cruel realities of War.

And this leads to the question whether the world might not have been a better world had the Germans taken to cricket and absorbed it as a national game.

Once at a dinner he gave me in Berlin, when the discussion was about various means of fostering a better understanding between England and Germany, I said to Herr von Ribbentrop:

'What about your people learning to play cricket up to Test Match standard? This would have a wonderful effect in the direction of the Führer's desires.'

I should add that at that time in 1934 Herr Hitler was anxious to promote a liberal 'exchange of youth' between the two countries and I had a long interview with him on the subject.

Herr von Ribbentrop shook his head, smiled mustard and replied: 'We should never learn to play cricket – too complicated a game for us.'

I argued oh! no. Cricket is essentially a pure Nordic game. They would probably produce a blond W.G. Grace. And anyhow the conventional technique of any athletic game would easily be acquired by so athletic a nation. Look at the standard of Lawn Tennis in Germany. Besides the thing that is difficult to acquire in cricket is not specialised skill in applying a peculiar club to a small red projectile but the fundamental quality required in all ball games. As for bowling, a nation which produces eminent hurlers of the discus and the javelin ought to raise any number of fast bowlers. What, too, about slinging hand grenades? And as for fielding, it would only take a few weeks to train a team of first-class catchers and throwers.

There was much argument round the table but I am afraid I did not convince the party.

I am afraid all the time I avoided the other side of the game – shall we call it, the moral aspect? I suddenly remembered a story told me by my young brother who once came back from Egypt in the same ship as the German Crown Prince.

My younger brother Walter, a brilliant pathologist, was a Major in the RAMC. He died in the awful typhus camp at Wittenburg in the Great War and he was the senior officer of six prisoners of war who volunteered for the perilous work. He had been taken with his field hospital at Armentières after Mons. The German doctors would not enter the camp except swathed in rubber armour, but they sent in our RAMC officers without any protection and short of all necessaries. There is a Memorial entablature to the dutiful valour of my brother and two other officers at the Millbank HQ of the RAMC.

However on the voyage home from Egypt was the Crown Prince who was returning from his tour in India. A gymkhana was arranged and the programme included a tug of war, Services v Civilians. My brother was 'anchorman' of his team. In the middle of the pull the Crown Prince, who was 'rooting' for the Services, suddenly had a bright idea. He ran forward and earnestly in a harsh whisper tried to persuade my brother surreptitiously to hitch the rope end round a convenient bollard.

'I was pretty puffed,' stated Walter, 'but I gasped out, that-wouldn't be-crick-et.'

I said, 'Anyhow, what do you know about cricket?' He said, 'Not as much as you, but more than Little Willie.'

I think Walter proved that he knew as much as there is to know about cricket – in that sense.

All the same I was, within limits, quite serious in my suggestion to von Ribbentrop and if ever I meet him again I shall remind him of it. And I shall, likely enough, if ever we get out of this present cul-de-sac of a catastrophe, offer to teach the Germans the game. I am sure I could make a job of them. I expect their best batsman would shape more like Tom Hayward than like Gilbert Jessop, and they would probably want to draw parallelograms of forces to work out the direction of the resultant for their off-drives.

But, as I say, I believe the Germans would produce good cricket. When I was over there in 1934 I saw some remarkable specimens of young Hitlerism. And what is more the young Germans can dance on the whole better than our young men think fit to bother about. This to me is significant because I happen to know that the real difficulty of batting, so far as style goes, is the acquisition and management of poise.

But I will not argue technical points today. I will write a book about the essential qualities of style later on, when the Siegfried Line is out of the way. I harbour the belief that there are many misconceptions about the inwardness of the meaning of such terms as style and orthodoxy and correctness and so on. The whole subject is thickly populated by ambiguities and by what our pals the logicians call 'question-begging appellatives'.

By the way, I believe my old and wakeful friend the Editor is adverting to my book, *Life Worth Living*, on another page of this valuable Annual. May I say that I had great difficulty about Cricket. I wanted to leave it out altogether because there was such a lot else to write about. So, indeed, it proved because when I had finished I had to sit down and cut out 40,000 words. But the publishers would not let me omit Cricket. So I thought best to include only reminiscences and valuations of such Test Match Cricket as had come my way. This unfortunately caused the non-inclusion of an immense amount of equally important memories – important at least in their personal interest for me – to do with some twenty full years of County Cricket and all the select excellencies of those notable matches called Gentlemen v Players. On the other hand there is the advantage that I can still some day write a book wholly about Cricket – to which that genius Neville Cardus has been exhorting me for years. Indeed so insistent was he, that I drew him a caricature of himself as a Secretary Bird, the bird with long legs and beak which cannot sing but can kill serpents.

(Annual, 1939–40)

BEHIND THE SCENES
By Ray Robinson

Left-hand batsman Ken Mackay pocketed a £1 note paid out by Australian vice-captain Neil Harvey.

It was the last side bet of the team's tour of 22 cricket matches and two baseball games in Africa.

Mackay, nicknamed 'Slasher' for his gum-chewing stolidity, had bet he would hit more sixes on the tour than dashing stroke-player Harvey. Rank outsider Mackay won – three sixes to one. Side bets like this are one of the ways in which touring cricketers beat the tedium of interminable playing, practising, packing, travelling and unpacking for nearly six months on end.

Since Qantas flew them from Sydney last October, they travelled 17,300 miles by plane, train, motor coach and car, criss-crossing South Africa and Rhodesia.

When the *Dominion Monarch* berthed in Sydney on Good Friday, New South Wales and Queensland players had exceeded 23,000 miles.

For £80 a month each and their keep, they had gone through Southern Africa unbeaten and earned about $25,000 for the Australian Board of Control and State cricket associations.

Between playing on 81 days they practised on 30 and travelled on 33.

After their struggle to save the first Test, they had to rise at 5 am the next day for an 800-mile flight to squeeze two Tests into 12 days.

Free days were so rare that when the Australians won the final Test ahead of time and I congratulated top-scorer Mackay on saving an extra day, he said dryly:

'Don't thank me – I'm more likely to prolong it a day.'

An Australian Appeal

... is usually loud, clear and unanimous. Above all it's enthusiastic! Australians enjoy their cricket as only sportsmen playing under ideal conditions can. There is always a warm welcome awaiting each new England Touring Team— and the promise of a hard fight. For those who decide to come and live in Australia there awaits an equally warm welcome—a welcome full of sunshine and the promise of a share in all that Australia has to offer.

The Ashes may change hands many times, but Australia's future is in *safe* hands.

Now more than ever Australia is batting on a good wicket!

For further information about life in Australia and details of a £10 passage, write today to:

CHIEF MIGRATION OFFICER, Dept. 95/58-96/58, AUSTRALIA HOUSE, LONDON W.C.2

(1959)

Only three of the 16 – Bob Simpson, Les Favell and Ron Gaunt – avoided injuries, which caused 40 calls to doctors and 19 X-rays.

Outside the sanctuary of the dressing-room one of the main activities is dodging ear-bashers wanting to talk cricket to players who get too much of it.

Few enjoy official cocktail parties, which the team must attend regardless of wear and tear on ear-drums.

More popular is a barbecue in a host's garden.

Unlike the mighty bowlers of the past who replaced lost moisture with beer, most of Ian Craig's team were teetotallers, except for toasts at functions.

Fast left-hander Alan Davidson, the bane of early batsmen, flung down nearly 3,400 balls on tomato juice and cool fizz.

At parties South Africans invariably lead top run-getter Jim Burke to the piano for a rock 'n roll session, with wicket-keeper Barry Jarman as vocalist.

Craig, wicket-keeper Wally Grout, and fast left-hander Ian Meckiff are the only regular smokers.

Fast right-hander John Drennan has a pipe or cigarette occasionally.

To escape ear-bashers at hotels, players haunt cinemas several nights a week or accompany hosts to clubs to play snooker.

Grout is the smoothest cueist, though Harvey twice recently cleaned up all the colours in one break.

The team's baseball stars were Harvey and Favell.

Harvey pitched through all nine innings in wins against combined South African nines at Johannesburg and Cape Town.

Between plays, catcher Favell repeatedly knocked his mask off for a breath of fresh air or a fresh word with an umpire.

If a pitch by Harvey cut the corner of the plate, Favell instantly dispelled the umpire's doubts by wagging the ball aloft with a triumphant yell of 'You beaut!'

Quiet and unemotional on the cricket field, Craig shed his restraint at first base to wave and shout 'One down – first to play!'

On free days, Craig often played tennis with Mackay, who was easily the team's best on the court.

Burke golfs off a handicap of eight, with long hitters Simpson and Meckiff.

None mastered the nap of the greens, which can cause putts to roll uphill.

Photographing lions, elephants, giraffes and other wild animals in Kruger and Wankie Game Reserves was the highlight of off-field experiences.

Though visitors are forbidden to get out of cars, Harvey could not resist climbing out to photograph a lion.

While he was busy, his companons suddenly noticed five lionesses padding up behind him.

Anxiously they called him to jump back into the car.

Before obeying, Neil took his last shot as calmly as he allows fast bumpers to whistle inches from his shoulders.

Harvey had the most vivid pictures, Drennan was the most enthusiastic photographer, and all-rounder Richie Benaud had a flair for the most artistic shots.

On the blistering Central African copper-belt 35 miles from the Belgian Congo, Meckiff, Drennan, Burge and Jarman wore yellow helmets with safety lamps down the copper-mine.

They found the sweating 2,300-ft level a better weight-reducer than a Turkish bath.

Several players – notably Melbourne school-teacher Colin McDonald and Benaud – gave up their spare time to visit schools to talk to hero-worshipping boys.

Successor to Bill Ponsford as the team's most successful fisherman, McDonald visited 12 schools, including the only Afrikaans-speaking primary school in Johannesburg where cricket is played.

Unlike most touring sides, Craig's team played no cards in the dressing room, but on 2,700 miles of rail travel two poker schools stopped only for meals and sleep.

Some train journeys made the Sydney-Brisbane run like a run around Luna Park.

Durban to Bloemfontein took 25 hours for 516 miles – shorter than Melbourne to Sydney.

Peter Burge was the train champion at poker. He is credited with a win every third telegraph pole, mainly by buying three for a full hand.

Non-punters in the team often contributed to a pool for investment by the few racegoers – chiefly Harvey, Burge, Favell and Jarman. This pool accounts for the winnings of some individuals being highly exaggerated.

Benaud and Favell's biggest bet – £100 to £25 – went amiss when the Rhodesian who laid 4 to 1 against Australia in the Tests, wrote to apologise for his inability to pay.

(1958)

A COMMENTARY BOX OF BAMBOO AND PALM
FRONDS . . .
By John Arlott

Idyllic is not a word commonly associated with commentary boxes, but it could be used without great extravagance of the structure that prompted these musings. Gray's Inn, on the north coast of Jamaica, was receiving a visit from an overseas team for the first time. The ground was, in a way, reminiscent of Swansea. On the north side, the road runs along the edge of the fence with the railway and Annotto Bay Station behind it, a couple of lazily swaying palms and then the whole distant sweep of the Caribbean, far bluer than the blue of Swansea Bay. But one nostalgic Welshman – Owen Davies, doyen of Jamaican umpires – muttered, again and again, 'St Helens – yes, yes – St Helens.'

The temporary stands were in place for the first time. More than three thousand people had paid a sum far greater than the club's coffers had ever known before – and to the rapture of the local children the Brigadier had flown in and landed his helicopter on the ground in front of the pavilion to watch the play. Not only was it the first broadcast ever made from Gray's Inn, but the Jamaican Post Office could not offer a lines service nearer than ten miles distant, so some very high frequency indeed was called for – with mixed success. But, for the visiting commentator, it was something of an occasion: the commentary box – or to be precise, squared arch – had walls of still green bamboo stakes and a roof of even greener palm fronds. What matter that elderly rum-punchers rumbled deeply at our backs, or that their juniors, leaping to their feet in excitement at every local success completely obscured the view of play? A commentary box of bamboo and palms, somehow, completed the circle.

Muffin man
Circles, fortunately, do not start, so this one may be broken at any point. We might come in at the point of no box at all. At the short-lived Ellis Park, which housed Tests at Johannesburg between the two Wanderers grounds, the commentator stood in the narrow strip between the boundary line and the crowd-fence with straps round his shoulders, carrying a board like a muffin man's tray with a microphone standing in the middle.

The roof-top positions at Cardiff Arms Park and St Helens, Swansea, used to be completely enviable when the sun shone, harsh places in the rain: emergency cover has removed the problem.

Immediately after the war, the pre-1939 box still clung to the wall opposite the scoreboard at Old Trafford. Bombing had blown away the handrail and most of the steps, and to see C. B. Fry, then in his seventies, swing his way up, monocle firmly fixed, binoculars swinging, was to know genuine admiration for the traditions of athleticism and the Royal Navy. Eventually, as had been threatening for years, a storm blew the old box down into the road behind – and splinters. Thereupon broadcasting was transferred to a hermetically sealed room in the scorebox: air has since been introduced mechanically.

Acute discomfort

Most commentary boxes, however, are one-night stand affairs, sited as a result of compromise between a BBC engineer and the ground secretary, each doing his best to preserve his own people's interests. In the days when a scorer was solely a Test match luxury, commentators were housed in little green wooden boxes with just sufficient room for one in comfort, two in acute discomfort. The commentator relied implicity on the scoreboard and endeavoured, when a wicket fell, to fill in his scorecard while talking about something else – or attempting to give the impression of repeating the facts at dictation speed for the listener.

In one such arrangement at Bath, the engineer had not appreciated that only one scoreboard maintained the running total and the individual scores of the batsmen. So when the commentary box was set down exactly in line with that board, there was no view at all of its highly relevant data. The scoreboard, built on huge trestles, looked as if it might be movable: at the expense of ricked back and a pulled thigh-muscle it was proved that two men could not move it an inch. After ludicrously elaborate experiments with mirrors, the eventual solution was for a friend to stand fractionally inside the boundary with a sideways view of the score, writing it down and turning it to the commentary box. Memory recalls, too, a weird, green, tarpaulin igloo at Leicester, wide open to the prevailing wind, which always seemed to prevail markedly on match days.

It compared oddly indeed with the present-day carpeted, board-room air of the box at Trent Bridge: the perfect, lofty view at The Oval: the intimate but roomy box at Edgbaston: the spacious, yet still poorly angled, viewpoint at Lord's: and the straight-down-the-pitch aquarium at Headingley.

Inches away

Yet the engineers themselves are probably proudest of the ingenious, fixed-in-a-jiffy, outside broadcast vans where, in a few minutes, steering wheel and all controls disappear under desk-tops, windscreens can be raised or closed and kept wiped, and a whole day's broadcasting can be recorded only inches away from the microphone or fed, on the instant of a distant cue, into services stretching to five continents.

Science – it's wonderful: but I hope the Leicester igloo has been preserved for the eventual museum of radio.

(1965)

An hour to go before my next commentary. Time to enjoy a pipe of St. Bruno . . .

the only tobacco which really satisfies me. St. Bruno has a very special flavour that I do enjoy. Yes, St. Bruno is a companionable tobacco . . . slow burning and satisfying.

You're bound to like

St BRUNO

The most popular flake of all

4'6 an ounce   0259 a

(1958)